Wesley Shank

THE IOWA CATALOG

Historic
American
Buildings
Survey

THE IOWA CATALOG
Historic American Buildings Survey

Wesley I. Shank

UNIVERSITY OF IOWA PRESS

IOWA CITY • 1979

Historic American Buildings Survey
Heritage Conservation and Recreation Service
Department of the Interior
Washington, D.C.

A List of Measured Drawings, Photographs, and Written Documentation in the Survey 1977

Acknowledgment is made to the Iowa State Historical Department, Division of Historic Preservation, Iowa City, for a grant toward the publication of this catalog.

Library of Congress Cataloging in Publication Data

Historic American Buildings Survey.
 The Iowa catalog.

 Bibliography: p.
 Includes index.
  1. Historic buildings—Iowa.   2. Iowa—History,
Local.   3. Architecture—Iowa.   I. Shank,
Wesley I.   II. Title.
F622.H57 1979   977.7   79–11666
ISBN 0–87745–091–9
ISBN O–87745–092–7 pbk.

Contents

Foreword

The historian's view of the brevity of the settlement period and subsequent development of Iowa is nowhere so tangibly demonstrated as in the buildings and structures which were created in the process. In virtually every county the first settlers, regardless of the style of homes they left to come to Iowa, followed a common pattern. They availed themselves of whatever building materials the environment and circumstance dictated; dugouts, sod, or logs. Their primary concern appears to have been shelter; functional, expedient, and spartan. Once established and able, however, their permanence and affluence were demonstrated by the construction of buildings following patterns well established in the communities from whence they came. Those people arriving after the brief settlement period brought new concepts and styles with them, adding variety to the community and neighborhood in which they settled. The impact of this continuous flow of ideas is easily observable in Iowa, if one has a key to understanding what occurred.

A handful of architects concerned with preserving this aspect of our heritage have, for more than 40 years, recorded these architectural forms under the auspices of the Historic American Buildings Survey. They have provided us with the key. It is sometimes stated that the cultural values of a people are reflected in their architecture. If this is true, then this book gives us the opportunity to consider the values of our ancestors as they are reflected in the buildings and structures preserved from our past in these pages.

Adrian D. Anderson
Iowa City, Iowa

Historic American Buildings Survey

THE Historic American Buildings Survey (HABS) is a long-range program to assemble a national archives of American architecture. Begun in 1933 by the National Park Service, in collaboration with the Library of Congress and the American Institute of Architects, the Survey represented one of the Federal government's first major steps toward the identification and preservation of historic structures. Since that time, thousands of records, consisting of architectural measured drawings, photographs, and written data, have been collected and deposited in the Survey's permanent archives in the Library of Congress. The structures selected for recording represent the full range of the American building art from the crude log cabin to the modern skyscraper and span the period between the first colonial settlements and the early twentieth century. Architectural interest and merit, as well as historical associations, are the basic criteria for the selection of buildings for the Survey.

The Survey is now a part of the Office of Archeology and Historic Preservation where it operates in cooperation with the other historic preservation programs of the National Park Service. John Poppeliers, Chief of the Historic American Buildings Survey, directs the recording program.

REPRODUCTION OF RECORDS

The Historic American Buildings Survey is one of the largest national collections of its kind in the world. It includes over 30,000 measured drawings, 45,000 photographs, and 22,000 pages of written historical and architectural data for over 16,000 buildings in the United States, Puerto Rico, and the Virgin Islands. These records may be consulted in the Library of Congress, Prints and Photographs Reading Room. Copies of any material in the archives may be purchased at stated prices by writing to the Library of Congress, Prints and Photographs Division, Washington, D.C. 20540. The most recent records are being temporarily held in the HABS office for editorial review; they are noted in this catalog by a dagger. Inquiries about obtaining copies of these records should be directed to the Historic American Buildings Survey, National Park Service, Department of the Interior, Washington, D.C. 20240. When ordering reproductions, buildings should be identified by the complete historic name (e.g., U.S. Courthouse and Post Office) and the assigned HABS number (e.g., IA–36).

The Historic American Buildings Survey archives contain documentation for 124 historic structures in Iowa. This documentation includes 146 architectural measured drawings, 456 photographs, and 489 pages of written historical and descriptive data that have been collected over a period of forty-four years.

HABS was created in the depths of the Great Depression with the two-fold purpose of assembling a centralized archives of the country's fast-disappearing historic architecture and providing as many jobs as possible for unemployed architects and draftsmen. The attempt to meet these two needs produced a program of such high standards and general usefulness that it was one of the few professional programs to be continued after the Depression.

The organization, funding, recording techniques, and historical emphasis of the HABS program have changed over the years, and the records for Iowa reflect the changes that have taken place nationally. Organization of the Survey program began in November 1933, and funds were made available in January 1934 under the Civil Works Administration. The national program was under the general direction of a small staff in the National Park Service which determined the general criteria for recording and set the standards of accuracy and quality for the records. Recording in Iowa was initially under the supervision of architect James A. Dougher, one of thirty-nine district officers who administered the HABS program regionally. It was the duty of the district officer to recruit architects, draftsmen, and photographers from the unemployment rolls, organize them into field teams, assign the buildings to be recorded, and approve the finished records. He was assisted in the assignment of work by a five-member advisory committee which drew up a priority list of recording projects to be undertaken. Special consideration was given to buildings threatened with demolition.

The district officer was nominated by the local chapters of the American Institute of Architects (AIA), and most of the field team members were also members of the AIA. Although a private professional organization, the AIA has cooperated with the National Park Service in conducting the Historic American Buildings Survey since its inception. A third cosponsor, the Library of Congress, receives and maintains the completed records. The library had itself taken part in some pioneering architectural recording projects and was a natural choice as the repository of the HABS collection. It was easily accessible to scholars, and reproductions could be ordered by mail from the library's Photoduplication Service, making the HABS collection available to interested persons all over the country. The requirement that all material in the archives be reproducible and the ready availability of reproductions are unique aspects of the Survey when compared to similar collections in other countries.

The first recording projects undertaken in Iowa reflect the Survey's continuing effort to document buildings that have an uncertain future, thus assuring that a graphic record of the building is preserved if the fabric itself cannot be. Among the buildings recorded in 1934 were the Pulver House in Vandalia, the Clegg House in Valley Junction, and the Barlow Granger House in Des Moines, all subsequently demolished. The William Maxson House in Springdale, where John Brown stayed, was ruinous when the HABS team measured and photographed it, but they were able to get enough information to prepare accurate drawings and preserve its image on paper. The Roelofsz (Viersen) House in Pella was demolished soon after an HABS photographer recorded it in 1934. These old photos proved useful when the city of Pella reconstructed the house as a bicentennial exhibition building forty years later. A recent example of eleventh-hour recording are the photographs made of the soon-to-be demolished Pottawattamie County Courthouse in Council Bluffs.

During the 1930s the men who formed the field teams were professional architects, and emphasis was, therefore, placed on measured drawings. Examples of the often elaborate delineation can be seen throughout this catalog. Less attention was given to photographic recording, and the photographs made during the 1930s—although interesting as historical records— are often not of high artistic or technical quality.

For the last twenty years, HABS field teams have been composed of architectural students and professors from schools across the country who are available during the summer university recess. They gain valuable professional experience while at the same time producing admirable drawings. Students from Iowa State University prepared the drawings of the First Evangelical Lutheran Church in Sheldahl.

Increased emphasis has been placed in recent years on recording by means of professional photographs and written documentation. Since hand measuring and drawing is time-consuming and costly, photographs can provide much broader coverage. In 1976 and 1977, HABS staff photographer Jack E. Boucher and contract photographer Robert Thall updated photographic documentation from the 1930s and recorded a number of previously undocumented buildings.

Although the Survey has a mandate to record buildings in all parts of the country, it has always been a small program with limited funds. Donations of both funds and records have been essential in providing for the growth of the collections. The Iowa records include several notable donations. In the 1960s the Des Moines architectural firm of Wetherell, Harrison, and Wagner donated measured drawings of the Little Brown Church in Nashua, the Sakulin Cabin in Des Moines, and the Hoover Birthplace and Friends Meetinghouse in West Branch. These gifts were the result of the generosity of William J. Wagner who also served on the National HABS Advisory Board.

In 1971–72 and 1973–74, the Iowa Arts Council, the Department of Architecture, and the Engineering Research Institute of Iowa State University jointly funded the "Studies of Historic Iowa Architecture." Twenty-three monographs prepared by project director Wesley I. Shank and his assistants David A. Petersen and John David Langholz were donated to HABS and greatly expanded and enriched the archives. In recent years, records have also been prepared by government agencies which find it necessary to demolish historic buildings in the course of their projects. The Reichard House in Knoxville was recorded by the Iowa Department of Transportation before it was removed for highway construction. The Clark House in Muscatine was documented by the Low Rent Housing Commission before it was replaced by apartments.

The Iowa records in the HABS collection are an important resource for anyone interested in the historic architecture of the state. However, this record is in no way complete. Many significant and well-known structures are not yet represented in this catalog. As funding permits and as groups willing to cosponsor recording projects can be found, documentation will continue to be added to the archives. It is hoped that the information presented in this catalog will encourage the identification, documentation, and preservation of more of Iowa's architectural patrimony.

THE IOWA CATALOG

In order to facilitate the use of the HABS collection, lists of the structures recorded have been published in catalogs from time to time. National catalogs appeared in the late 1930s and in 1941; and a supplement to these was issued in 1959. The rapidly increasing size of the HABS collection has subsequently made a national catalog impractical. As a result, in 1963, the first in a new series of state and regional catalogs was published. This volume is a part of that series. It is a catalog of buildings in Iowa recorded by the Historic American Building Survey from 1933 to 1977. It was compiled by Professor Wesley I. Shank of Iowa State University who visited almost all of the recorded structures to ascertain their present appearance and condition. Based on these observations and long years of study of Iowa architecture, Professor Shank provided the introduction which broadly outlines the development of architecture in the state, illustrated with examples drawn from the HABS records. It should be made clear that this catalog is not a definitive listing of worthwhile historic architecture in the state, but rather a guide to materials in the HABS collection. While it contains entries for many of Iowa's most significant structures, numerous important buildings remain to be recorded, and new entries will be added as recording continues.

Each entry gives a concise physical description and historical account, and lists the number of HABS records for each documented structure. Organization of the entries is geographical by city. Within cities the entries are arranged alphabetically by historical name with cross-references to current or commonly used names. Buildings in rural areas are listed as being in the vicinity of the nearest town or city. Addresses and locations have been given as accurately as possible so that this catalog may serve as a guide for visiting the listed buildings. The format for each entry is as follows: the historical name; HABS number; address; brief description, including construction materials, dimensions, number of stories, roof type, and important interior and exterior details; date of erection; architect, if known; alterations and additions; important historical facts; and a listing of the number of measured drawings, photographs, photocopies of old views, and pages of written data available in the HABS archives.

In addition to HABS recording, some of the listed buildings have been declared National Historic Landmarks (NHL), and some have been placed on the National Park Service's National Register of Historic Places (NR), either as individual buildings or as part of an historic district. These designations are noted by the appropriate initials following the entry.

Appended to the catalog is a separate listing of the Historic American Buildings Survey Inventory forms for Iowa. These brief one-page forms are on file in the Library of Congress where they form a companion collection to the HABS records.

December 1977

The following are abbreviations and symbols used in this catalog:

IA–24	Historic American Buildings Survey number. All buildings recorded by the Survey are assigned an HABS number. These numbers should be used when inquiring about a structure or ordering reproductions.
Sheets	Sheets of architectural measured drawings.
HABSI form	Historic American Buildings Survey Inventory form. A brief one-page form on file at the Library of Congress.
NR	Indicates that a building has been placed on the National Register of Historic Places of the National Park Service. If the structure is part of an historic district, rather than individually designated, the name of the district appears in parentheses.
NHL	Indicates that a building has been declared a National Historic Landmark by the Secretary of the Interior. National Historic Landmarks are automatically listed on the National Register of Historic Places.
ext. and int.	Exterior and Interior.
†	A dagger after a date indicates that the records made on that date are being temporarily held in the HABS office for editing. Inquiries about these records should be sent to the Historic American Buildings Survey, National Park Service, Department of the Interior, Washingon, D.C. 20240.
*	An asterisk preceding entries in "The Iowa Catalog" indicates that the building is illustrated in Wesley I. Shank's essay "Historic Architecture in Iowa" or in Todd Mozingo's "A Survey of Styles."
photocopy	Photographic reproductions of old maps, sketches, drawings, photographs, etc.

Historic Architecture in Iowa

Historic architecture in Iowa began with the laying out of the land in patterns of settlement and the constructing of the log cabins and other simple buildings of the pioneer period, which may date from the 1830s to as late as the 1870s, depending upon the time at which the particular locality was first settled. Pioneer buildings were replaced as soon as possible; the period was short. Most of the first permanent buildings were plain and unpretentious in appearance, their design and construction following custom and tradition. Buildings such as these are often called vernacular architecture. A small number of buildings followed the architectural styles current elsewhere in the country.

Accompanying the penetration of the railroad network into the state and the end of the Civil War, the new technology of industry began to appear and bring about important changes in life and architecture. New and more complex types of buildings were required, architects were trained to design them, the construction industry was set up to build them, and the newly harnessed agricultural and commercial wealth of the state supplied the money. These new buildings expressed this new society by means of the architectural styles current in the older settled portions of the country. The account of the difficulties encountered as these changes came about is interesting, instructive, and often humorous. It may be the most important lesson to be learned from a study of the history of Iowa architecture.

In the first two decades of the twentieth century, Iowa architecture, in a small number of its buildings, had moved out ahead of the rest of the country. As part of a region of several states centering on Chicago, Iowa was the location where several buildings by Louis Sullivan, Frank Lloyd Wright, and their followers were built. These architects, who are now usually identified as the

Prairie School, had attained an important original architectural expression of midwestern American life and contributed to the worldwide development of modern architecture.

In this essay, historic architecture after the pioneer period will be divided into three periods. The first will be called the pre-Civil War period, although its concluding date will be taken as the year the Civil War ended, 1865. The technology of this period was, in general, preindustrial. The second will be called the post-Civil War period and will span from 1865 to 1900. During this time industrial technology was introduced. The third period includes the first few decades of the present century and will be called the Early Twentieth Century. In some parts of the state settlement occurred late enough so that there are few or no examples of pre-Civil War buildings. Before considering architecture, however, this essay deals first with the ways towns and rural areas were laid out.

Unfortunately, only a small amount of information about the historic architecture of Iowa has yet been gathered, and only tentative observations may be made at this time. Nevertheless, the writer hopes that the essay and its illustrations, the catalog section, and the Survey of Styles will make a useful presentation of this information.

EARLY SETTLEMENT

The history of settlement in Iowa and the factors which determined where cities were located and on what pattern cities and rural areas were laid out forms an important background to the understanding of the historic architecture itself.

Iowa was settled as part of the general movement of the American frontier westward and northward following the rivers upstream from the neighboring states of Illinois and Missouri (Fig. 1). Through the Louisiana Purchase of 1803, the land that was to become Iowa was added to the United States, but was not officially opened to white settlement until 1833, when a fifty-mile-strip just west of the Mississippi River was purchased from the Sac and Fox Indians after the Black Hawk War of 1832. Similar purchases followed in 1835, 1845, and 1852, which effectively cleared the area of Indians and permitted white settlement all the way to the Missouri River. A remaining portion of the land along the northern border of the state was purchased and opened for settlement in 1856. Meanwhile, political development was taking place. The Iowa Territory was formed in 1838 from land that had successively been part of the Louisiana Purchase, of the Michigan Territory, and then of the Wisconsin Territory. In 1846 statehood was achieved. The speed of settlement was astonishing. Within little more than ten years after the state was opened for settlement, the population had reached 40,000, and by 1850 it was close to 200,000, a rate of increase greater than that in any neighboring state with the exception of Wisconsin.[1]

Good farmlands were the chief attraction for the first settlers. With soils among the best in the world, Iowa remains predominantly an agricultural

2

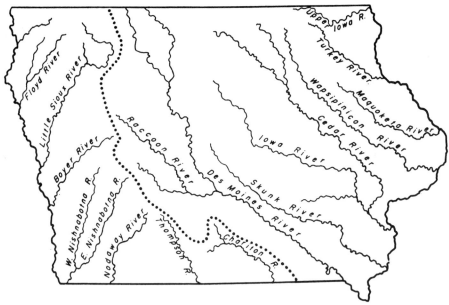

Fig. 1. Iowa's major streams. The dotted line is the water divide between the Mississippi River and Missouri River drainage. Used by permission from *A History of Iowa* by Leland Sage © 1974 by The Iowa State University Press, Ames, Iowa 50010.

state. Most of the land is flat or gently rolling, and much of it was originally grass covered; but there were woodlands too, providing timber for construction. Limestone was available in many localities, but only in a few of them was it suitable building stone. The winters were rigorous with snowfall and three or four months of frozen ground, and the summers were hot with dependable rainfall. Because the rivers offered an economical means of transportation and because the wooded land, as was found near the rivers, was preferred to the more distant grasslands, which were thought to be infertile, the first settlements were attracted to locations on the Mississippi River at the east boundary of the state and the Missouri at the west, and later along the several rivers which flow diagonally from the northwest to the southeast and into the Mississippi.

Several factors influenced where cities and towns were located in Iowa. Some of the most important ones can be identified, and for any particular settlement it must be kept in mind that usually a number of factors were operating. A frequent factor, as mentioned above, was the presence of a river, providing access to water-borne transportation and to water power for gristmills and sawmills. Sometimes this factor operated first to attract the mill, around which the town later grew up. A second factor attracting towns, and also serving as a nucleus for them, was the presence of Indian Agencies or United States forts, as was the case with Agency, Fort Dodge, and Des Moines (originally called Fort Des Moines). The choice of a location for a county seat or state capital was a third factor, responding in varying degrees to politics and to

3

the need to be central to the area to be served. This factor was in part responsible for the laying out of Iowa City in 1841 as the territorial capital, later to become the first state capital. Overland transporation routes constituted a fourth factor influencing town location. At first they consisted of stagecoach routes and trails, but in 1855 the railroad was added as it entered the eastern portion of the state. During the ensuing development of the railroad network —it did not reach the western boundary of the state until 1867—existing towns vied with each other in offering inducements to attract the railroads and, in addition, the railroads themselves created towns and sold rural land along their rights of way, profiting by the sales and then by the supply of customers near the tracks.

Regardless of location in the state, however, the street pattern of nearly all the towns followed a rectangular grid that was sometimes modified slightly to relate it to the topography. Many towns established before the Civil War centered on a public square and had all of their lots of a uniform and spacious size (Fig. 2). But many nineteenth-century towns laid out after the Civil War followed a different pattern. They lacked the public square and centered instead on a business district identified by its narrow lots (Fig. 3). Outside of the business district, the larger lots of the earlier period were still used. In both periods, the principal streets were often wider than the others, and alleys crossed all the blocks, providing access to the rear of the lots.

Fig. 2. Original plat of Des Moines.

4

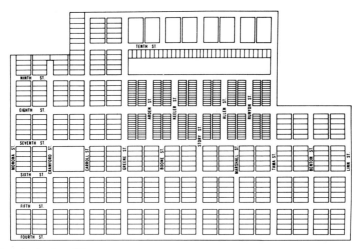

Fig. 3. Original plat of Boone.

Although showing only limited variety in pattern, the town plans in Iowa usually responded to the geographic features of the land, paralleling a river or avoiding a ravine or a bluff. Much less flexible was the pattern on which farmlands were laid out. The Land Ordinance of 1785 had established a north-south east-west coordinate system which divided the land into square townships that were six miles on a side and contained thirty-six sections, each a mile square (Fig. 4). Thus rural roads ran north-south and east-west at one-mile intervals. This rational system facilitated the identification, buying, and selling of parcels of land, the principal purposes for which it was established. But often the boundary lines and roads thus established bore no relationship to the topography—to streams, the slope of the land, the characteristics of the soil—nor to the social needs of the people. According to the Homestead Act of 1862, a settler in order to obtain a grant of 160 acres (a quarter section) had to live on it for five years. Thus farmhouses were built on the farms, isolated from towns and often from near neighbors. For American settlers who had been accustomed to similar farms farther east, this pattern led to a lonely, although familiar, existence. For European immigrants used to living in villages and going out daily to their fields, the effects of such isolation and loneliness were often extreme. One historian cites the Homestead Act as the direct cause of the high incidence of insanity among all rural people in the Middle West during the nineteenth century.[2]

In Iowa, the settlement pattern followed by the Amana Colonies provided a significant exception to the isolation and loneliness that accompanied the rural settlement pattern of the Middle West. A German Christian utopian-communitarian society known as the Community of True Inspiration built six villages in Iowa County in the late 1850s and spaced them along a road one or two miles apart—East Amana, Amana, Middle Amana, High Amana, West Amana, and South Amana. Here the people lived, with the community barns grouped at

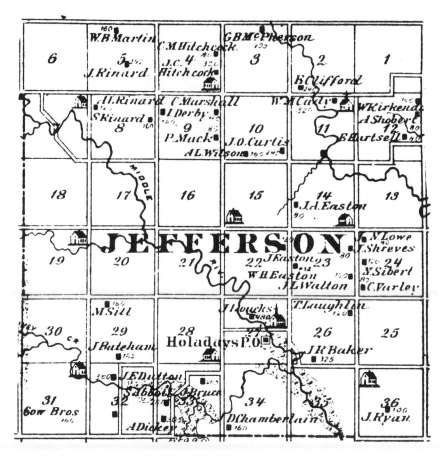

Fig. 4. Jefferson Township, Adair County. Shows typical layout of a section in one-mile squares. Reproduced from A. T. Andreas, *Illustrated Historical Atlas of the State of Iowa* (1875), with permission of the·State Historical Society of Iowa.

the village edge, went out to their fields to farm and returned at night (Fig. 5). The village pattern seems to have been used because it suited the practical nature of the people and their communal way of life. But other settlers in America, a large percentage of whom were European immigránts, might also have chosen to live in villages or towns had not the Homestead Act required them to live isolated from one another on their own farms.

PIONEER BUILDINGS

Whether in rural locations or in towns, the first buildings in an Iowa settlement had to be cheap, fast, and simple enough for any pioneer to build. Log cabins were the rule, but occasionally, it is believed, plank cabins were built. Both took the form of plain boxes with gable roofs. Few survive. Most were replaced soon, as intended, and the rest rotted quietly into oblivion.

Fig. 5. West Amana. View of the town from the south. Photo Robert Thall 1977.

Three well-known types of log cabins are found in Iowa, identified by the type of corner joint. In the first, built quickest, the logs were left round and fit together at the corners in crudely cut saddle-lap joints. The crevices between logs were filled with clay and small stones. The First House in Fort Des Moines of the 1840s and the Rowland Gardner Log Cabin in Arnolds Park of 1856 are examples.[3] The second type of log cabin construction is found in the Alexander Young House, relocated in Washington, Iowa, and dating from the 1840s. Here the logs were squared up, and at the corner, the joints have been cut with the top of each log peaked like a gable roof and the bottom shaped to receive the peak of the log below. This kind of joint sheds water better than the saddle-lap joint, but it leaves wider spaces between the logs to be chinked. The Mars Hill Baptist Church, built in the vicinity of Floris in the middle 1850s (Figs. 6, 7), is an example of the third type of construction, in which the logs were hewn square and the corner joints ingeniously formed in self-draining dovetail joints.[4] These joints directed any entering water to the outside and allowed the lengths of the logs to be closer to one another, reducing the amount of chinking required. This third type of construction is the most durable of the three, all of which may be traced back to early Scandinavian settlers in Delaware and Germans in Pennsylvania, although in Iowa it is also possible that later Scandinavians and Germans may have reintroduced the log cabin in the nineteenth century.[5]

A plank cabin which has survived—restored after having been modified considerably—is the Herbert Hoover Birthplace House at West Branch (Figs. 8, 9), built about 1870 by Jesse Hoover, the president's father. Having only two heated rooms and an unheated back porch, the house was built with exterior walls of board-and-batten siding and interior walls of vertical boards without battens. The boards were the only weight-bearing vertical members in the walls, a very economical method of construction. A wood stove served for heat and for cooking.

Fig. 6. Floris vicinity. Mars Hill Baptist Church. Photo Robert Thall 1977.

Fig. 7. Floris vicinity. Mars Hill Baptist Church. Interior. Photo Robert Thall 1977.

Fig. 8. West Branch. Herbert Hoover Birthplace House. Courtesy of the Herbert Hoover National Historic Site.

Fig. 9. West Branch. Herbert Hoover Birthplace House. Interior view showing plank wall construction. Courtesy of the Herbert Hoover National Historic Site.

Compared with the buildings of the pioneer period, those of the pre-Civil War period were larger and more complex in their planning and construction. Towns and farmsteads looked as if the new settlers had moved in to stay. Traditional practices in building design and construction were usual. It is an interesting fact of the period that recent European immigrants often followed the traditions of their mother country. Less usual were buildings in the architectural styles of the period—Greek, Egyptian, Gothic, and Romanesque Revivals, and the Italianate style. For these buildings there was often a designer who might have been a skilled builder or an architect, and there were several instances where the building technology of the period was not able to construct and equip such buildings properly.

We will look first at domestic architecture. In 1836, Judge David Rorer—who later became a prominent attorney in his town—built a brick house for himself in Burlington (Fig. 10).[6] Said to be the first brick house in Iowa, the building was very plain, probably a simple rectangle in plan containing only two rooms. It had the stepped gable-end walls common in brick buildings of the time. Another plain early house, also a simple rectangle in plan but somewhat larger, is the Pearson House, built in Keosauqua in 1845 (Fig. 11), with its lower story of limestone and its upper one of brick. This house is still standing, although

Fig. 10. Burlington. Judge David Rorer House. Date of photo unknown.

Fig. 11. Keosauqua. Pearson House. Photo C. C. Woodburn 1934.

the Rorer House is gone. However, in the old section of the Mormon built town of Nauvoo, in nearby Illinois across the Mississippi, one may still see many simple brick buildings of this time. They would have been substantially the same in the adjoining parts of Iowa.

Probably houses like the Rorer House and the Pearson House were not uncommon in Iowa at the time, as their simplicity suggests. However, many other houses are found which appear to follow a T- or an L-shaped plan characteristic of farmhouses, but found in town houses as well, suggesting that the patterns of rural and urban family life did not differ greatly. In these houses the kitchen and its smaller related rooms form a rear wing at one side or at the middle of the main part of the house. An excellent example of this farmhouse plan is the Daniel Nelson House on a farm north of Oskaloosa, with its barn opposite it across the road (Fig. 12). The main portion of the house is two stories high, and on each floor there is one room on each side of a central hall. The kitchen wing at the rear is one story high, forming the wing of an L-shaped plan. Wall construction is of brick, and heating and cooking were by means of fireplaces. The house dates from the early 1850s. Another example of the farmhouse plan is found in the Hancock House in Bentonsport (Figs. 13, 14, 15, 16, 17). Construction is in wood frame, but the floor plan is quite similar to that of the Nelson House, except that the one-story kitchen wing spreads across the whole width of the rear of the house. Cooking was by stove, and heating by both stoves and fireplaces. It also dates from the early 1850s. A larger version of

11

this floor plan has a central hall with a front and a back room on each side of it, on both stories of the main portion of the house, as seen at the Farm House, built 1860–65 and now a museum on the Iowa State University campus in Ames. This house was originally used as the residence of the superintendent of the model farm that was part of the state agricultural college. Here the kitchen wing at the rear of the L-shaped plan had a second floor, although its roof was lower than that of the main portion of the house. Heating and cooking were by stoves, and until an extensive turn-of-the-century remodeling, the brickwork of the walls was exposed. Milens Burt of Muscatine prepared plans for this house and its barn. He was described as "architect and builder, a prudent, judicious, and excellent mechanic." Since the design of the house followed the traditional design of the type that builders produced, it would seem that Burt was an architect who had learned his skills as a builder. Such builder-architects were common in the nineteenth century. William Foster in Des Moines was another. The Bernhart Henn House, built in Fairfield in 1857–58, is similar to Farm House in massing.[7] It was a simple two-story block, of generous proportions, with a service wing at the rear. The roof of the main portion was hipped, and in this respect it differed from the three houses of farmhouse plan just mentioned. For those three, the roof of the main portion was a gable roof, and the houses were entered on the eave—that is, the long—side. The Henn House's hipped roof was crowned with a low lantern, the walls were red brick, and the stone-linteled windows were regularly spaced. Parsons College bought the house and conducted its first classes there in 1875 and later named the building Ewing Hall.

Fig. 12. Oskaloosa vicinity. Daniel Nelson House. Photo Robert Thall 1977.

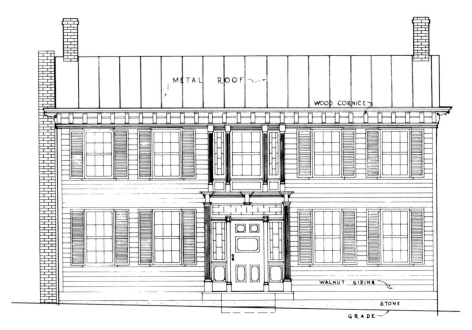

Fig. 13. Bentonsport. Hancock House. West elevation. J. B. Chambers, delineator.

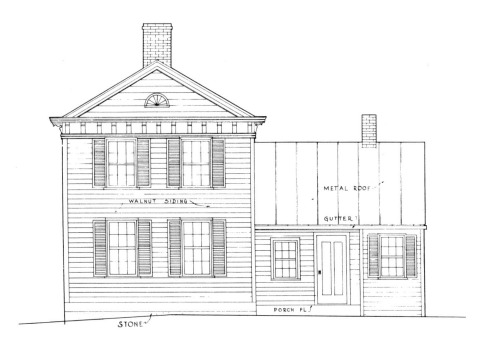

Fig. 14. Bentonsport. Hancock House. South elevation. J. B. Chambers, delineator.

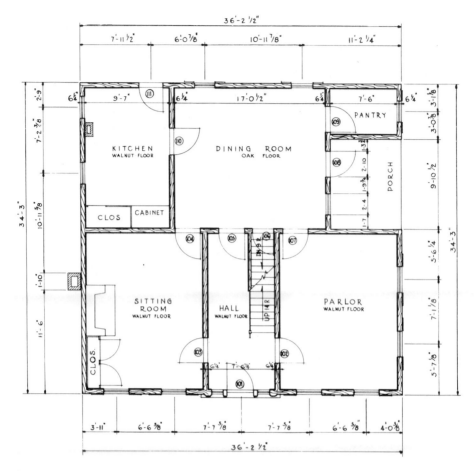

Fig. 15. Bentonsport. Hancock House. First floor plan. J. B. Chambers, delineator.

Four other buildings of the period provide examples of other house plans which were used before the Civil War. These plans were different from one another and from those already described. One of them, although a hotel, is included here because of its domestic character. This is the Western Hotel (Figs. 18, 19, 20), still standing near the town of Holy Cross and once providing a stopping place for travelers about twenty miles west of Dubuque. Built on a hillside site in about 1850, its rooms were regularly disposed, and both attic and basement rooms were utilized. The next two buildings were in south-central Iowa and do not survive. One was the Pulver House (Figs. 21, 22, 23) in Vandalia, built about 1848 of wood-frame construction above a stone basement recessed into the hillside. Basement rooms may have been used as workshops. The rooms of the main floor are grouped without any corridor, and most have doors communicating with the exterior and with adjoining rooms. The plan is unusual. The other was the Barlow Granger House, which stood on a hill southeast of Des Moines. Built in 1856, the original portion of this brick house

14

was quite small and compact; but after it was enlarged the house had no corridors and, as in the Pulver House, one had to walk through one room to reach another. Granger was the publisher of the first newspaper in the city, politician, lawyer, and businessman.[8]

The last building is known as the Bucknell House (Fig. 24). It still stands in Decorah and is reputed to have been built in 1855 by a builder by the name of David Reed. The house is unusual for two reasons: its walls were constructed of concrete, not a common building material for that date (they are scored to resemble stonework, and the eaves and porch columns were decorated with bold scrollwork jigsaw work, since removed); and the house was an early example of a multiple dwelling, for it contained three separate complete dwelling units.

From these houses of the period, we can identify some characteristics of the technology of Iowa's pre-Civil War architecture. Windows provided natural light and ventilation, desired in warm weather but in the form of drafts and air leakage, unwanted in the cold weather. Artificial lighting was provided by oil lamps and candles, and the light of the fire in the fireplace. During the period, the methods of heating were changing. Fireplaces had been the traditional method, and they were built under early pioneer conditions and in permanent

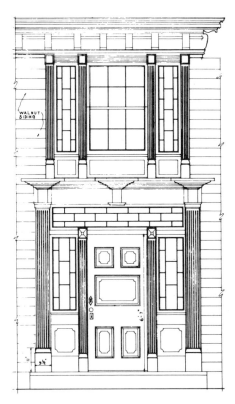

Fig. 16. Bentonsport. Hancock House. Detail of main entrance. J. B. Chambers, delineator.

Fig. 17. Bentonsport. Hancock House. Front entrance. C. C. Woodburn 1934.

15

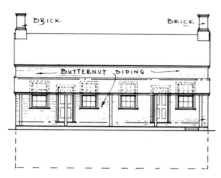

Fig. 18. Holy Cross. Western Hotel
(Pin Oak Tavern). East elevation.

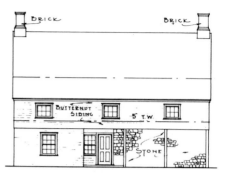

Fig. 19. Holy Cross. Western Hotel
(Pin Oak Tavern). West elevation.

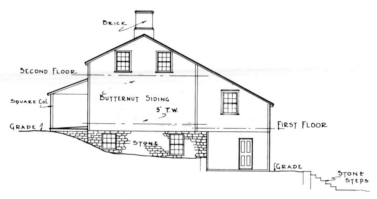

Fig. 20. Holy Cross. Western Hotel (Pin Oak Tavern).
North elevation. Carl W. Buechele, delineator.

dwellings as well. By the 1830s Count Rumford's improvements in fireplace design were beginning to be generally known in the United States, so that more heat could be obtained from fireplaces, and chimneys less often smoked into the rooms. However, stoves heated much more efficiently than fireplaces, were more convenient for cooking, and were beginning to replace fireplaces for both purposes. Thus during this period, we find both fireplaces and stoves. The former are seen at the Nelson House and at the Western Hotel. The Hancock House has both fireplaces and stoves, and in the Pulver House, the Bucknell House, the Granger House, and Farm House stoves seem to have been used for both heating and cooking, although a cellar workroom in the Pulver House contained a fireplace, and there was one in what seems to have been an addition to the Granger House. Food was stored in caves adjoining the cellars of both the Pulver and the Granger House, and the cellar of the Granger House included a fruit room, a well, and a cistern for the kitchen. None of these buildings had indoor sanitary facilities. Toilets were in outhouses.

Fig. 21. Vandalia. Pulver House. Photo C. C. Woodburn 1934.

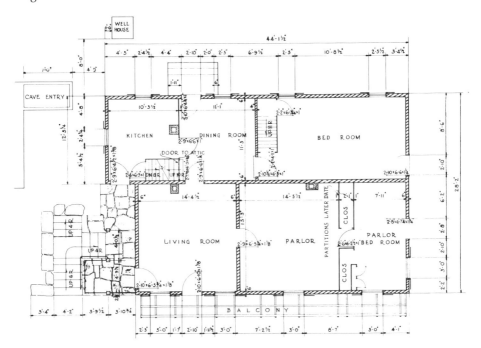

Fig. 22. Vandalia. Pulver House. First floor plan. J. B. Chambers, delineator.

17

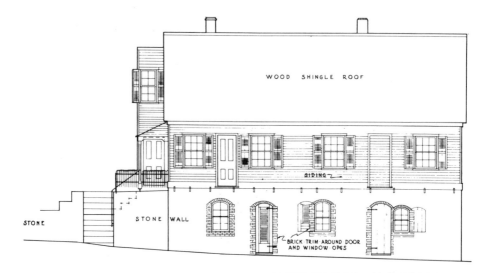

Fig. 23. Vandalia. Pulver House. South elevation. J. B. Chambers, delineator.

Some of the most interesting pre-Civil War domestic architecture in Iowa is found in the buildings built by recent European settlers following the practices of their native countries. The town of Pella, for example, was settled in the late 1840s by immigrants from the Netherlands, and a few buildings survive which identify this heritage. The Van Spankeren House (Figs. 25, 26)—a boyhood home of Wyatt Earp—has the large windows found in the Netherlands and the same plank-and-beam floor construction found in seventeenth century Dutch buildings in New York and New Jersey, ultimately derived from the Netherlands. On Washington Street are the Central College Temporary Quarters, which have tumbled brick at the sloping edges of the gable, reflecting Dutch construction practices (Figs. 27, 28). Another European tradition, believed to be that of Luxembourg, is represented in the Stephen Frank House (Figs. 29, 30, 31), one of several similar houses on a street at the west side of the town of Saint Donatus, originally called Têtes des Morts. The simple stone house is unusual for its hipped-gable roof, the fine carved entrance that it once had, and the barn which was attached to one side of the house when it was recorded in 1934.

The buildings of the Amana Colonies should be mentioned here because of this people's German cultural heritage. As we have seen with the villages, the planning of the buildings also responded strongly to the particular needs of this community. For example, in the houses each person was provided with a bedroom and a sitting room, and there was in addition a common sitting room for each family, but the kitchens and dining rooms were omitted because the community dined together in common dining halls and the meals were prepared in communal kitchens.[9, 10] For construction, brick, stone, and wood-frame were all utilized, often in different portions of the same building. For ideological reasons, the builders of the Community of True Inspiration produced simple designs for its houses and provided equal and ample accommodations for everyone. It was decided that, in the long run, sound construction was the most economical. Stoves were used for heating. In general, however, the architecture appears to lie within the broad tradition of the American vernacular tradition of the time. The German influence may lie only in the craftsmanship and the execution of the details of construction. The W. M. Moershal House in Amana, bearing the date 1858 carved in its west gable, is a picturesque example (Fig. 32).

All of the houses mentioned may be considered examples of vernacular architecture. Their design is orderly, simple, and usually symmetrically balanced. Openings in exterior walls are uniformly spaced and, in two-story buildings, second-floor openings are usually placed above those of the first floor. Doors, single windows, and chimneys are usually centered on the wall of a room. If a wall has two windows, they are symmetrically and evenly spaced on it. The over-all volume of a building is simple and sheltered under a single-roof form, with only porches or the kitchen—if it is in its own wing—protruding. This system of architectural order derives from the architectural principles of the Renaissance as they became traditional in Europe and then in its American colonies. In its details, vernacular architecture is simple, with decoration omitted or greatly simplified. When occasionally an attempt is made to include decoration, the result is usually naive, as in the Hancock House. Here the dec-

Fig. 24. Decorah. Bucknell House. The elaborate wooden porches have been removed. The original stucco was scored to resemble stone. Photo LeRoy Sampson 1934.

19

orative framing of the front entrance and the windows directly above it, the cornice, and the mantel provide charming examples (Figs. 16, 17).

Some of the houses in Iowa at this time followed the architectural styles, of which the Greek Revival was common. The William Maxson House, built in mid-nineteenth century on a farm east of Springdale (Figs. 33, 34, 35) is an example. The heavy wooden cornice and the paneled doorways with straight transoms and side lights are typical Greek Revival features. But here the designer or builder encountered a problem which he solved poorly. He seems to have felt that he had to center the attic windows at each gable end of the house and that he had to center the two chimneys there also, which thus obstruct the passage of light and air through the windows. The conflicting requirements were not resolved. (This stone house is historically significant because John Brown and his followers were quartered in it during 1857 and 1858 while training for the raid on Harpers Ferry, West Virginia, carried out in 1859.[11])

With paired brackets at the eaves and a lantern at the peak of its main hipped roof, the Rensselaer Russell House in Waterloo (Fig. 36) is an example of another architectural style of the pre-Civil War period, the Italianate style. Russell, a businessman from central New York State, kept a detailed ledger of his expenses of construction while the house was being built from 1862 to 1863. He

Fig. 25. Pella. Van Spankeren House (Wyatt Earp House). Photo Robert Thall 1977.

appears to have superintended the construction. The designer is not known. For this time in Iowa, builders' pattern books may have been the source for a house such as this.

Fig. 26. Pella. Van Spankeren House (Wyatt Earp House). Dining room showing exposed plank-and-beam construction of second floor. Photo Robert Thall 1977.

Fig. 27. Pella. Central College. Temporary Quarters. Photo Robert Thall 1977.

Fig. 28. Pella. Central College. Temporary Quarters. Detail of east gable showing tumbled brick. Photo Robert Thall 1977.

Fig. 29. St. Donatus. Stephen Frank House. Detail of carved entrance door.

Fig. 30. St. Donatus. Stephen Frank House. North elevation with attached barn.

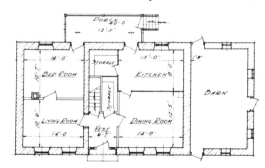

Fig. 31. St. Donatus. Stephen Frank House. First floor plan. Herbert A. Kennison, delineator.

Fig. 32. Amana. Moershal House. Photo Robert Thall 1977.

Fig. 33. Springdale. William Maxson House (John Brown House). East elevation.

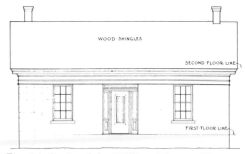

Fig. 34. Springdale. William Maxson House (John Brown House). South elevation. C. C. Woodburn, delineator.

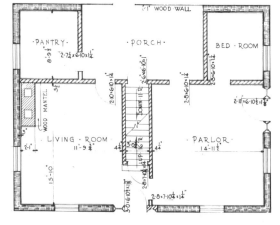

Fig. 35. Springdale. William Maxson House (John Brown House). First floor plan. J.B. Chambers, R/A, delineator.

Fig. 36. Waterloo. Rensselaer Russell House. Photo Robert Thall 1977.

The Edward Langworthy House in Dubuque (Figs. 37, 38, 39), built in the late 1850s, is an example of the work of an architect, John Francis Rague, who had come to Dubuque in 1854 to practice.[12] Langworthy, a native of New York, was one of the first settlers in Dubuque and, with several brothers, had been prominent and successful in business, banking, the lead industry, and politics.[13] The house, following an octagonal plan with an octagonal lantern capping the roof and a lower service wing to the rear, was sited on high ground and was visible from the city of Dubuque and the Mississippi River to the east. Seen close up, the brick walls are found to be visually broken up by tall bay windows and by an entrance porch with columns of octagonal cross section capped by a bracketed cornice—all in wood. The design is skillfully carried out.

Further consideration of the buildings of John Francis Rague takes us to the next group of buildings—government and institutional buildings. Rague had received his training as an apprentice in the architectural office of Minard Lafever in New York, the usual kind of architectural training for the time. Before designing any work in Iowa, Rague had designed and supervised the construction of the former Illinois Capitol in Springfield, begun in 1837. Subsequently he designed the Territorial Capitol in Iowa City (Fig. 40), whose construction was begun in 1840. Meanwhile a wood-frame building had been completed in Iowa City to provide a temporary meeting place for the Territorial Legislature in 1841. Late in the following year the legislature was able to meet in Rague's

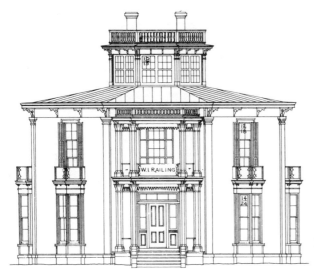

Fig. 37. Dubuque.
E. Langworthy House.
South elevation.

Fig. 38. Dubuque. E. Langworthy House. West elevation.
Harry N. Bevers, delineator.

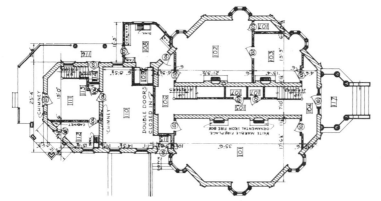

Fig. 39. Dubuque. E. Langworthy House. First floor plan.

building, although final completion of it did not come for several years.[14] A fine example of the Greek Revival style and closely resembling the former Illinois Capitol, the building was constructed of local light gray limestone. On its long sides, pedimented Greek Doric porticoes in wood emphasize the central entrances. A tall domed central tower, also of wood, crowns the roof, and in the central hall a graceful spiral stairway leads from the ground floor to the legislative chambers on the second. When Iowa became a state in 1846, the building became the first state capitol, and in 1857, when Des Moines was designated as the capitol city, "Old Capitol" was given to the state university, now the University of Iowa, for whose campus it remains an architectural focus. The Temporary Capitol in Des Moines built in 1856–57 served as the second state capitol from 1857 to 1886. It was a three-story rectangular brick block in the Italianate style.[15]

In practice in Dubuque, Rague designed two more governmental buildings. One of these was the City Hall for Dubuque (Fig. 41), built in 1857–58 following the general pattern of Faneuil Hall in Boston. The ground floor was a public market subdivided into stalls, each provided with a gas outlet for lighting and a flue for a stove for heating. Cast iron columns were used at this level, the floor construction of the building was timber, and the exterior walls were brick. City offices and chambers were on the second floor, and the unobstructed space on the third floor was used for social events, celebrations, and dances. The decoration of the building exterior consisted of paired brackets at the eaves, the expression of the structural bays by means of simple blind arcades in the brickwork, and a no-longer extant tower of elaborate design rising from the ridge of the roof near the east end of the building.[16] The other governmental building by Rague was the Dubuque County Jail (Fig. 42), also built during 1857-58. Its planning was typical for county jails at the time. The front portion of the building, a block two stories high, consisted of a house and offices for the sheriff. The jail adjoined the rear of the house and was of the same height, but included three tiers of cells within that height (Fig. 43), and a well-lit and well-ventilated spacious indoor exercise area. Thus the sheriff could supervise the jail day and night. Rague designed the exterior of the building in the Egyptian Revival style, one of the less often used architectural styles of the period, sometimes used for prison architecture. The walls were of solid stonework, but most of the exterior architectural detailing, with the exception of the wooden cavetto cornice, was of metal.[17]

In response to the manifestations in Iowa of two nationwide trends—a public awareness of the need for the humane treatment and care for the insane and the development of the asylum as a public institution as the means of providing that care and treatment—probably the largest and most complex building in the state during the period was built. This was the Iowa Insane Hospital at Mount Pleasant (Fig. 44) begun in 1855, the first of four state mental hospitals to be built by the first years of the twentieth century. In connection with their responsibilities for the hospital at Mount Pleasant, a commission of Iowa citizens visited several mental hospitals east of the Mississippi and then engaged the Boston architect Jonathan Preston, who had been recommended by some of the foremost American authorities on insanity. He designed the building with two central structures, the front one housing administrative offices and the rear one housing the kitchen, bakery, dining room, chapel, and other common facilities. Symmetrically placed wings were joined to either side of the central structure, the men's wards on one side and the women's on the other. There were enough rooms in the wards so that patients could be grouped according to their particular classification of illness, in order to improve care and treatment. Handcars in the cellar carried food from the central kitchen to dumbwaiters connecting with the several individual dining rooms in each wing. Interior walls contained built-in ducts for heating and ventilating air circulation. The design followed the early 1850s policy statements of the Association of Medical Superintendents which, in effect, sought to cure insanity by creating a social and physical environment within the asylum, which would correct the deficiencies of the community environment from which the inmates had come and which was believed to have been the cause of their insanity.[18]

Although a competent architect designed the building, poor construction practices and the substitution of inferior materials clearly indicated that the

Fig. 40. Iowa City. Old Capitol (Third Territorial and First State Capitol).

building technology in pre-Civil War Iowa was inadequate for such a major construction project. However, the state legislature in its actions gave no indication that it recognized the need for a higher level of technology. This pattern of events recurred in the construction of several other buildings for public institutions during the nineteenth century, and Mount Pleasant provides a typical instance. The basement of the building was constructed of a poor quality of stone, improperly laid, so that cracking in the upper parts of the building developed and extensive replacement of stone was required. Toilets and bathrooms were built of inadequate materials, a fact which became most obvious as water and filth penetrated plastered walls and ceilings below. Brick interior wall and floor construction had to replace the earlier wood-framed floor and walls. Although the architectural style of the building was described at the time as Elizabethan, it appears so only in the use of label moldings above the windows. The bracketed eaves and orderly massing more strongly follow the Italianate style, and it is from the over-all massing of the elements of the building and from the over-all size, some seven-hundred-sixty-feet long and an average of three stories in height, that the main architectural impact was derived.

An Iowa firm of builder-architects, Robert S. Finkbine and Chauncey F. Lovelace, prepared the plans and specifications for a smaller state institutional building, the Iowa Institution for the Education of the Blind at Vinton (Fig. 45), following a simple version of the Italianate style with almost classic restraint. Their work appears to have closely followed the recommendations of the institution's board of commissioners. Curiously enough, the building seems to have had no special features for the blind. The central portion was built in 1858–62, and two wings were added to it during the next fifteen years. Only one problem developed, but it was one which recurred in other buildings. The steam-heated, circulating-air heating system which was originally recommended was not installed. To save money, stoves were substituted for it, and they did not heat the building. Around 1866 they were replaced by a hot-air furnace, which also proved inadequate, and a system like the one originally recommended was finally installed, using an engine-driven fan to circulate the heated air.

A certain lack of differentiation among buildings with respect to their use of space was often found in the architecture of the mid-nineteenth century and earlier as well. In effect, buildings which differed little from houses seem to serve nondomestic purposes. Two college buildings point out the distinction clearly. One of them is Pioneer Hall (Fig. 46), the original college building at Iowa Wesleyan College at Mount Pleasant, built in 1843–45. In floor plan and in general appearance this red-brick building could easily be taken for a house, and in fact was used as one for awhile. Originally, however, it was built to provide classrooms and residential apartments for college faculty. In part, the lack of differentiation in architecture at this time may be attributed to the simple technology followed and to the fact that it was usually not necessary to provide accommodations that would be safe for gatherings of a greater number of people than might be found in someone's house. The needs of this society were modest compared to ours. The second example is "Old Main" (Fig. 47), a red-brick Italianate style building adjacent to Pioneer Hall and constructed in 1854–55. With its imposing block-like appearance it could not be mistaken for a house, nor would it in fact be possible to use the building conveniently as a house. A simple rectangle in plan and three stories in height, the building had central corridors with staircases at each end which allowed large numbers of people to enter and leave its classrooms quickly and safely. "Old Main" was designed expressly to be a college building and contrasts sharply with its undifferentiated predecessor nearby of only a decade earlier.

Fig. 41. Dubuque. City Hall. Photo Jack E. Boucher 1977.

In the case of buildings designed for religious worship, differentiation was usually present, that is, these buildings took their form from their particular spatial and expressive needs. The Little Brown Church in the Vale in the vicinity of Nashua (Fig. 48) is an example. Built in 1860 and originally called the First Congregational Church of Bradford, its Gothic Revival exterior, with

30

steeply pitched roof, pointed arches at door and windows, and tower standing at the entrance, suggests an English medieval stone parish church. Once inside the building, however, the visitor sees wallpaper, dark-stained woodwork and pews, coal-oil lamps, a rotating fan suspended above the pulpit, and a pressed-metal ceiling. The impression is overwhelmingly one of mid-nineteenth century rural America.

The restored Quaker Meetinghouse at West Branch (Figs. 49, 50), dating from about 1860, also follows a characteristic form, recognizable for what it is and following the floor plan used in such buildings for over a centruy. The long rectangular building is entered on one of its long sides through two doors, the one for men at the right and the one for women at the left. The congregation sat on several rows of pews facing the other long side, where ministers, elders, and elderly Friends sat on two rows of pews facing the congregation. At each end of the building there was a stove. Crossing the room and dividing it into two equal parts was a wooden partition which could be opened at eye level by raising a series of shutters. During worship services the shutters were open, women sitting on the left side and men on the right. During business meetings, however, the shutters were closed so that the men and women could meet separately.[19] Of wood-frame construction with white clapboard siding at the exterior and plastered interior surfaces, the building was simple because of the

Fig. 42. Dubuque. Dubuque County Jail. Photo Jack E. Boucher 1977.

Friends' requirements for simplicity in a house of worship. Relocated from its original site in the town to a place near the Hoover Birthplace, the building draws its historical significance from the fact that Herbert Hoover attended meetings there as a boy.

Also of simple design were the meetinghouses of the Amana Colonies, in whose large, plain rooms men, women, and children worshipped separately. These meetinghouses were usually placed in the center of a residential block, with houses grouped at the street frontage (Fig. 51).

The Shot Tower, built in Dubuque in 1856, is a rare surviving example of a type of industrial structure prevalent in its time (Figs. 52, 53). Lead, mined in the vicinity, was made into shot by allowing molten drops to fall from the top of the tower into a container of water at the base. Two mills furnish additional examples of industrial buildings common during the period. Built from 1851 to

Fig. 43. Dubuque. Dubuque County Jail. Interior showing cells. Photo Jack E. Boucher 1977.

1853 to utilize the waterpower of the Upper Iowa River, the City Stone Mill in Decorah was a gristmill and continued operation by waterpower until the 1940s (Fig. 54). The West Amana Flour Mill (Fig. 55), a clapboarded wood-frame structure dating from 1860 and built in West Amana, was originally water powered, but was later converted to steam power. This mill served farmers within a twenty-mile radius and sold flour to people outside of the Amana Society. The mill no longer stands; it was dismantled.[20]

Fig. 44. Mount Pleasant. Iowa Insane Hospital. Aerial perspective ca. 1892.

Fig. 45. Vinton. Iowa Institution for the Education of the Blind (now called Iowa Braille and Sight Saving School). Copy of old postcard after 1913 remodeling.

Fig. 46. Mount Pleasant. Iowa Wesleyan College. Pioneer Hall. Photo Robert Thall 1977.

Fig. 47. Mount Pleasant. Iowa Wesleyan College. Old Main. Photo Robert Thall 1977.

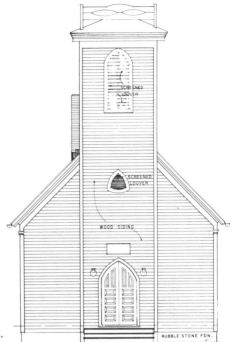

Fig. 48. Nashua. Little Brown
Church in the Vale. East elevation.

Fig. 49. West Branch. Quaker Meetinghouse. View showing partition dividing men's
and women's sections. Courtesy of the Herbert Hoover National Historic Site.

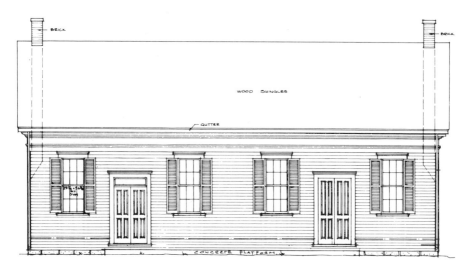

Fig. 50. West Branch. Quaker Meetinghouse. West elevation. William J. Wagner, delineator.

Fig. 51. Amana. Main Meetinghouse. Photo Robert Thall 1977.

Fig. 52. Dubuque. Shot Tower.
Photo Jack E. Boucher 1977.

Fig. 53. Dubuque. Shot Tower.
Conjectural restoration of top.
Harry N. Bevers, delineator.

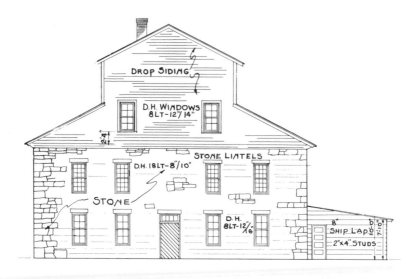

Fig. 54. Decorah. City Stone Mill. South elevation. Bertram R. Olson, delineator.

Fig. 55. West Amana. Flour Mill. Photo C. C. Woodburn 1934.

During this period—1865–1900—several significant changes occurred in Iowa architecture. As individual fortunes were accumulated, a small number of fashionable, ostentatious mansions appeared, along with many smaller houses expressing the similar aspirations of the middle class. The growing governmental needs of the state were expressed in the construction of many substantial and impressive county courthouses. The increasing number of social responsibilities allotted to government was seen in the continuing construction of institutional buildings for education and for care. The appearance of the railroad station and the tall office building indicated significant changes in the economic development of the state.

In order to meet these new architectural needs, the college-trained architect appeared along with the general contractor, both as we know them today, and the technology of constructing and equipping buildings caught up to the demands made upon it.

The architectural styles of the period have in common the accentuation of verticality. Thus, doors, windows, columns, towers, and even roofs were tall and narrow. Also, the styles contained elements freely combined and borrowed from the historical architecture of the past. The Second Empire style was characteristic, taking its elements from the French Baroque. Similar in general appearance, but using instead elements from Gothic architecture, was the High Victorian Gothic style. The Gothic Revival and the Italianate styles continued from the previous period. Buildings for government tended to follow a style based on the Renaissance or on ancient Rome. A Romanesque style of France inspired the prominent Boston architect H. H. Richardson, and his was the first American style to be widely followed. Less obvious was the fact that, although the decorative architectural details of these buildings were indebted to the past, in other respects these buildings were, in general, new solutions to the new architectural requirements of a new society. There were no historic precedents for the floor plans of its college buildings, mental hospitals, county courthouses, railroad stations, tall office buildings, or even its mansions.

A most interesting and, as historic architecture, probably the most important house of the post-Civil War period in Iowa is "Montauk" (Figs. 56, 57), built in 1874 in Clermont for William Larrabee, who was governor of the state during the late 1880s and a crusader against rate abuses by the railroads. The house is virtually as it was when the governor and his family lived there, with their furniture, books and papers, musical instruments, paintings, statuary, and souvenirs from their world travels still to be seen—a clear expression of success in Victorian terms. Standing near the edge of a bluff and overlooking the town, the house is an Italianate red-brick block, with generously bracketed eaves, and windows following a variety of arched forms, most having limestone hoods. From the working drawings, the name of the architect has been found to be Edward Townsend Mix of Milwaukee.[21]

Fig. 56. Clermont. Montauk (Gov. William Larrabee House). Photo Robert Thall 1977.

With "Montauk," "Terrace Hill" in Des Moines and the Grenville Dodge House in Council Bluffs are among the most elaborate examples of post-Civil War houses in the state. The latter two were designed by W. W. Boyington, a prominent Chicago architect of the time. "Terrace Hill" is probably the most luxurious nineteenth-century house in Iowa (Fig. 58). It was completed in 1869 for B. F. Allen, a wealthy Des Moines financier. Frederick M. Hubbell, a successful Des Moines insurance magnate, bought it in 1884, and the house remained the property of the Hubbell family until 1971, when it was presented to the State of Iowa to become the governor's mansion. Crowning a hill which, when the house was built, lay to the west of the city, the four-story tower of the house commands a wide view of the city.[22] Slate-covered mansard roofs and brick walls with concrete quoins and window hoods and other architectural decorations of varied lineage are as lavish as the fine woodwork and extensive decoration within the house. In Council Bluffs, the house of Grenville Dodge, transcontinental railroad magnate, is similar to the Hubbell mansion, was built at about the same time, but is on a smaller scale (Figs. 59, 60). The architectural style of both of these houses is Second Empire, of which the mansard roofs are the hallmark.[23]

All three of these houses are products of fortunes accumulated through the opportunities offered on the American frontier. The houses were intended to express the social status which their owners had achieved, a social status which, since it did not rest upon family or hereditary privilege, as such things did in Europe, craved ostentatious expression of wealth as a substitute for gentility and culture, hardly qualities through which the fortunes had been made. One suspects that the nineteenth century magnate and his wife may at times have felt uncomfortable in their palatial residence, although their children, growing up in its luxurious surroundings and having had the approved education purchased for them, probably felt quite at home there.

The luxury of these three houses included new domestic conveniences, such as running water, bathrooms, and indoor toilets. Both "Montauk" and the Dodge House were built with central heating systems, although in most of the rooms of Montauk the precaution was taken to install thimbles through which a stove pipe could be connected to a chimney in case stoves had to be brought in because the central heating had failed. At "Terrace Hill," however, stoves and fireplaces were used for heating until Hubbell bought the house and installed a central heating plant. For artificial illumination, oil lamps were originally used at Montauk, and manufactured gas at the Dodge House, where the fuel had just become available upon completion of the house.[23, 24]

Three more brick houses, smaller and less ostentatious, show nevertheless the same desire to express the wealth of their owners. The earliest, built in Burlington ca. 1866, was the home of Judge Charles Mason, who had been the

Fig. 57. Clermont. Montauk (Gov. William Larrabee House). Parlor. Photo Robert Thall 1977.

41

first chief justice of the Supreme Court of the Iowa Territory and who later became prominent as manager of several important financial enterprises in that city (Figs. 61, 62). The Ralph case of 1839, which granted freedom to a former slave who went into the free Iowa Territory with his master's permission, was tried in Mason's court. The next house was built in 1871 in Fort Dodge for James Swain, a wholesale and retail druggist, and was bought in 1879 by Webb Vincent, who with his associates experimented with gypsum from the local deposits and invented and pioneered the use of gypsum wall plaster (Fig.63).[25]

Fig. 58. Des Moines. Terrace Hill (Allen-Hubbell House). Photo Robert Thall 1977.

Fig. 59. Council Bluffs. General Grenville M. Dodge House. Photo Robert Thall 1977.

Both the Mason and the Swain-Vincent houses follow the Second Empire style. The third house, which follows the Italianate style, was built in the early 1870s for Simeon E. Dow, who made his fortune in western Iowa through land speculation (Fig. 64).

Believed to have been built in 1865, the Clegg House (Fig. 65), which formerly stood in Valley Junction (now called West Des Moines), was an octagon-plan house whose walls were built of gravel concrete, following the ideas of Orson Fowler, who advocated the use of this building material because it was cheap and available everywhere, and who advocated the octagonal plan form because the resulting compact volume of such a house would be economical to heat.[26] The Clegg House, whose floor plan closely followed one of Fowler's published plans, was an example of economical housing for people who had to put comfort and practicality first. The philosophy behind the source of the design of houses like the John Reichard House (Fig. 66), which stood until recently near Knoxville, was similar. Although the house was built in 1864 or 1865, it followed the pattern of the Gothic cottage advocated twenty years earlier by A. J. Downing as an appropriately unpretentious and economical substitute for the large Greek Revival farmhouses that then dotted the rural landscape of New York. The style of the Reichard House would be called Carpenter Gothic today, because of its wooden scrollwork decoration at the eaves and the front porch. The floor plan was the typical farmhouse plan of the pre-Civil War period.

Most of the religious buildings which were recorded by HABS in Iowa for the post-Civil War period are examples of vernacular architecture. The Hicksite Friends Meetinghouse that stood in Marietta is such an example, as are the Methodist Episcopal Church near Gilbert, the First Evangelical Lutheran Church in Sheldahl, and the Chapel of Saint Anthony near Festina. The exterior of the meetinghouse resembled that of the meetinghouse at West Branch of about 1860, already mentioned. Although the Hicksite Friends were a conservative faction of Quakers, Quaker meetinghouses generally followed the same floor plan, and so it may be reasonably assumed that the floor plans of the two examples in Iowa were similar to each other.

 . At a rural location east of Gilbert and near the South Skunk River, the Methodist Episcopal Church of Milford Township, now called the Pleasant Grove Church, resembles many country Protestant churches of the period (Fig. 67). It is a simple gable-roofed clapboarded box, with its architectural decorative features limited to a few moldings. The date of construction was 1873 or 1874. The First Evangelical Lutheran Church, now called the Sheldahl Norwegian Lutheran Church, in the Town of Sheldahl is also a one-room church, but

Fig. 60. Council Bluffs. General Grenville M. Dodge House. Interior after 1916, showing parlor with original furnishings. Courtesy Union Pacific Railroad.

although built in 1883 it looks as though it had been built at least fifty years earlier (Fig. 68). Pastor Osmund Sheldahl, who was one of the owners of the land on which the town of Sheldahl was platted, built the frugal little church and made the furniture himself with the help of his sons and some friends. He owned the building and preached in it. Only the paneled pulpit and the turned balusters of the communion rail relieve the stark simplicity of the plank interior walls; the clapboarded exterior is utterly plain.

Fig. 61. Burlington. Judge Charles Mason House. East elevation. Charles L. Ritts, delineator.

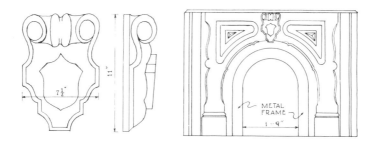

Fig. 62. Burlington. Judge Charles Mason House. Decorative details. Paul Haskell, delineator.

Fig. 63. Fort Dodge. Swain-Vincent House. Photo Robert Thall 1977.

Fig. 64. Dow City. Simeon Dow House. Photo Robert Thall 1977.

Fig. 65. West Des Moines. Clegg House. Photo C.C. Woodburn 1934.

Fig. 66. Knoxville vicinity. John Reichard House. Photo John Hotopp 1976.

Reflecting the concept of a holy place, rather than that of a place of religious assembly, the tiny Roman Catholic Chapel of Saint Anthony (Fig. 69) was built near Festina in 1885, said to be in fulfillment of a vow which a French mother made to secure her soldier son's safe return from military service during Napoleon III's Second Empire. With walls of rubble stonework and miniature tower and steeple of wood, this church seats only eight people.[27]

Contrasting sharply with the vernacular architecture of the religious buildings just mentioned is that of Grace Cathedral (now Trinity), the Episcopal cathedral in Davenport (Figs. 70, 71). The building is noteworthy because its architect was Edward Tuckerman Potter of New York, who designed in the High Victorian Gothic style then popular in the United States—partly as the result of Potter's work. Potter had received the office apprenticeship type of training in architecture, as had John Francis Rague mentioned earlier. Potter's apprenticeship had been with Richard M. Upjohn, well-known Gothic Revival architect of the pre-Civil War period in New York.[28] The cathedral was under construction from 1867 to 1873. Its walls are of rock-faced yellowish limestone, and its nave is spanned by dark-stained wooden trusses whose lower members are laminated wood arches. A clerestory hardly a foot in height and a series of very small dormer windows provide unexpected spots of colored light overhead. Rather low and long for its height and very human in scale, the cathedral is picturesquely sited on a broad expanse of lawn reminiscent of an English cathedral close.

Fig. 67. Gilbert vicinity. Methodist Episcopal Church of Milford Township (now called Pleasant Grove Church). Photo Wesley Shank 1972.

Fig. 68. Sheldahl. First Evangelical Lutheran Church (now called Sheldahl Norwegian Lutheran Church). Photo 1974.

Fig. 69. Festina.

St. Anthony's Chapel.

North elevation.

Bertram R. Olson, delineator.

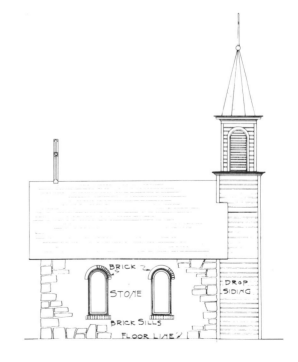

BRICK

STONE

BRICK SILLS

FLOOR LINE

DROP SIDING

Several government buildings of the period are represented in the HABS collection. Their histories illustrate a wide range of circumstances under which public buildings were then designed and constructed.

The Franklin County Courthouse in Hampton, built 1866–68 and predecessor to the present courthouse, was designed by Usiah Weeks, a contractor, who worked closely with the county board of supervisors in preparing the plans and specifications. Weeks's low bid gave him the contract for construction. The building was a simple stone rectangular gable-roofed volume, with offices and vaults on either side of a central corridor on the first floor, and with a large assembly room occupying most of the second. The gable ends of the building were expressed as a pediment, and there was a low tower and cupola at the ridge of the facade, all a late example of the Greek Revival style of architecture.

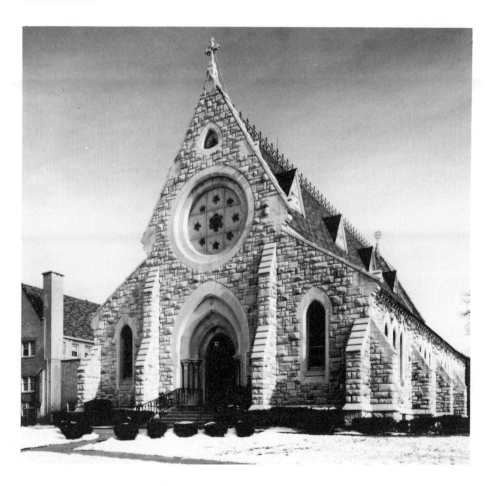

Fig. 70. Davenport. Grace (now Trinity) Episcopal Cathedral. Photo Jack E. Boucher 1977.

Fig. 71. Davenport. Grace (now Trinity) Episcopal Cathedral. Interior. Photo Jack E. Boucher 1977.

The Boone City Hall was constructed through separate contracts for the various portions of the work—stone foundation, carpentry, roof—except that the brickwork was done by day labor working under a superintendent. Unlike the Franklin County Courthouse, there was no general contractor, and it is not known who performed the role of general supervision and organizing of the work. Possibly the building committee or the City Council themselves took care of it. The city hall is essentially a two-story downtown commercial building of the kind found in any Iowa town. The upper floor, with decorative brickwork arcading and round-arched windows, housed the city functions. The ground floor, with doors and display windows formed in an arcade, which looked a bit awkward with its alternation of narrow and wide arches, was designed as rental space. The dates of construction are 1873–74, and the name of the designer is not known.

The designer of the Madison County Courthouse, which stands in the center of the town square in Winterset, is known (Fig. 72). He was Andrew H. Piquenard of Chicago, who is also one of the architects of the present Iowa Capitol in Des Moines. The courthouse was built in 1876–77. With light-beige ashlar walls, a central, domed tower of pressed sheet-metal fastened on an iron framework, and a fire-resistant floor system of shallow brick arches supported on iron beams, the courthouse follows a Greek cross floor plan, with a portico and entrance at the end of each arm of the cross. One architectural historian has aptly called courthouses like this "county capitols" because they look like small versions of state capitols.[29] The building was erected by a superintendent of construction who was hired by the Board of Supervisors and paid an annual salary. He had the power to purchase materials and to employ workmen and laborers to complete the work, and he was directly responsible to the Board.

Since Iowa has so many fine nineteenth-century county courthouses of the post-Civil War period, it is appropriate to mention some examples of two prominent architectural styles which many of these buildings follow. One of the styles follows classic Roman or Italian Renaissance inspiration; this is the county capitol type. The Marshall County Courthouse in Marshalltown (Fig. 73), like the Madison County Courthouse just described, is an example. Built in 1884–86, it was designed by John C. Cochrane of Chicago, partner of A. H. Piquenard, and with him one of the architects for the present state capitols in Des Moines and Springfield, Illinois. The other prominent architectural style was the Richardson Romanesque, named after its originator, the prominent Boston architect H. H. Richardson, who took his inspiration from the French Romanesque style. In Iowa, the Montgomery County Courthouse, built in Red Oak in 1890 (Fig. 74), and the Clinton County Courthouse (Figs. 75, 76), built a few years later in Clinton, are two examples in this style. Both buildings have walls of rusticated stonework in which color is an important aspect of the design—deep reddish and cream-colored stone for the first building and reddish-brown for the second. Both have picturesque commanding towers.

The last illustration of late nineteenth century government buildings is the United States Courthouse and Post Office in Des Moines, known when it was razed in 1968 as the Old Federal Building (Fig. 77). It was built in two phases. The original two-story building was designed by Alfred B. Mullett, supervising architect of the United States Treasury, and was built in 1867–71. In 1885–90, a third story was added to this building and a three-story addition extended it to the rear. The later work was designed by Mifflin E. Bell, also in the post of supervising architect. Both the original and the enlarged building had Joliet limestone walls with reserved classical detailing at the doors, windows, stringcourses, and cornices, all crowned with an imposing mansard roof. The architectural style was French Second Empire, well known in government

Fig. 72. Winterset. Madison County Courthouse. Photo Robert Thall 1977.

Fig. 73. Marshalltown. Marshall County Courthouse. Photo Robert Thall 1975.

buildings from Mullett's State, War, and Navy Building completed in Washington, D.C., in 1871. Although the Des Moines building was modest by comparison, it utilized the best fireproof construction practices of the time. Competent building contractors were not yet available in Des Moines in 1867, so Mullett hired his own superintendent of construction, who in turn hired and supervised day labor to construct the building, and who could thus keep construction costs in line and assure quality workmanship. By 1885, contracts for the different portions of the work were entered into, but still the federal government did not deal with a general contractor responsible for the construction of the whole building.

The histories of the design and construction of several buildings for state institutions during the period furnish considerable information about the development of the architectural profession and the building industry. At the beginning of the period, neither was capable of meeting the new demands of such large and specialized buildings. By the end of the period, design and construction could proceed quickly and efficiently, with a minimum of problems.

Attempting tasks far beyond his abilities, John Browne of Des Moines accepted the commission as the architect of the first college building on the Iowa State University campus (Fig. 78). He appears to have been capable neither of designing the building nor of preparing the necessary working drawings for its construction. The excavation was begun under his direction;

Fig. 74. Red Oak. Montgomery County Courthouse. Photo Robert Thall 1977.

Fig. 75. Clinton. Clinton County Courthouse. Photo Jack E. Boucher 1977.

Fig. 76. Clinton. Clinton County Courthouse. Interior. Photo Jack E. Boucher 1977.

56

the basement walls were built as little more than thin stonework lining the sides of the excavation. Worthless, these walls had to be removed and replaced. Browne was dismissed and a more competent architect, Charles Dunham of Burlington, replaced him early in 1865. He properly designed the building, and construction was completed in 1868. Containing virtually all of the State Agricultural College, as the institution was then called, including the president's offices, classrooms, museum, library, students' rooms, dining hall, and kitchen facilities, the building was of brick, three stories high with mansard roofs and towers flanking the facade—a bastion of learning on the rural prairie. Problems with the heating system developed and were mishandled in the same manner as at the school for the blind at Vinton. Another problem was discovered when the building sewer was investigated and was found to have been built so that its contents did not flow, but instead had collected for nine years under one of the wings of the building. The supervision of construction had been lax, it would appear. In addition, the fire resistance of the construction was poor. After destructive fires in 1900 and 1902, the building was razed.

Fig. 77. Des Moines. U.S. Courthouse and Post Office (Old Federal Building). View of light well in north section of building. Photo Mark A. Knudsen 1968.

Fig. 78. Ames. Iowa State University. College Building as it appeared from 1868–76. Courtesy Iowa State University Library, Special Collections.

Two additional state institutional buildings begun during the decade of the 1860s offer further insight into the process of building design and construction during this time. The first is the Iowa Institution for the Education of the Deaf and Dumb (Fig. 79), built at Council Bluffs beginning from 1868 and continuing to 1880, and also destroyed by fire in 1902. Schwarz and Dilger of Springfield, Illinois, were the architects, selected after a competition among several architects for the commission. A. J. Davis of New York, one of the foremost American architects of the pre-Civil War period, was among several unsuccessful competitors for the job. As constructed, the building had its administrative and common facilities at the center, with matching wings at either side for males and females. Construction began under a general contractor who was incompetent. His price for the work had been unrealistically low, and he went bankrupt. He used unseasoned wood for floors, doors, and windows, so that winter air entered readily and made heating impossible after the wood had shrunk. The other state institutional building, the Iowa Hospital for the Insane at Independence (Fig. 80), was the second state mental hospital to be built in Iowa. It was designed by Stephen V. Shipman, architect then of Madison, Wisconsin, and later of Chicago, and was under construction from 1868 to 1884. The period of construction here was long, as was the case with the School for the Deaf and Dumb, because the state legislature appropriated funds only for small increments to be completed at a time. Although the general contractor for the first portion of the mental hospital also went bankrupt, work had been competently done. The state took over construction, hiring its own superintendent, who was well qualified. The building, with its gabled and mansard roofs and its echelon plan of wards flanking the central portions of the building, remains in use today.

With the Iowa Hospital for the Insane built at Clarinda (Fig. 81) in 1884–99, we have an indication that Iowa architects had become successful competing with out-of-state architects for the large institutional commissions of the period. The architects for this hospital were the firm of Foster and Liebbe of Des Moines. William Foster was a builder-architect, and Henry F. Liebbe, his German-born partner and former employee, had learned his trade from Foster. In its general planning, the hospital resembles the earlier state mental hospitals. In style, it is essentially Eastlake, which made use, both inside and outside of buildings, of carved and turned wooden decorative forms.

In the last decade of the nineteenth century appear the first buildings by Iowa architects who had received academic training in architecture. Of the Cedar Rapids firm of Josselyn and Taylor, Henry S. Josselyn was a graduate of the Massachusetts Institute of Technology program in architecture, and Eugene Taylor had graduated from Grinnell College in Iowa and had taken courses in architecture at M.I.T. This firm designed Morrill Hall (Fig. 82), built in 1890–91

Fig. 79. Council Bluffs. Iowa Institution for the Education of the Deaf and Dumb. Main Building. Photo ca. 1887. Source: *Council Bluffs, Iowa: Illustrated* (1887).

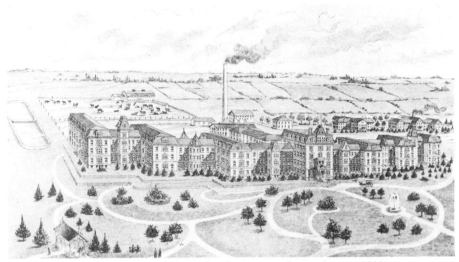

Fig. 80. Independence. Iowa Hospital for the Insane. Engraving ca. 1891.

on the Iowa State University campus. The building housed several different activities. The most difficult one to provide for was the museum. Because of the fire hazard of the alcohol in which museum specimens had to be stored, it was necessary to construct a fire wall to separate the museum, laboratories, and other related rooms from the library and the chapel, which were also part of the building. Ventilation needs were met by four chimneys which did not serve fireplaces, but used the natural draft as a means of exhausting air from the parts of the building. Heating was by steam, and lighting was by electricity. A Romanesque arcade and tower, and a tall slate-covered roof with Queen Anne pediments are well integrated in this eclectic design. In Morrill Hall we have an example of a building in which the scope and quality of professional architectural services and the work of the general contractor were essentially what they would be today for such a building. The efficiency with which these services were performed was in sharp contrast with the great difficulties which had been experienced in the construction of the College Building on the same campus twenty-five years earlier. The firm's design for the Hospital for the Insane at Cherokee, built in 1896–1902, is similar in its combination of varied eclectic elements (Figs. 83, 84). This was the last of the four state mental hospitals to be built. It follows the same extended floor plan used in the other three. Here, as was the case at the hospital in Clarinda, motor-driven fans are part of a heating and ventilation system for the whole building.

Two characteristic building types which originated in the nineteenth century are the railroad station and the skyscraper. At Council Bluffs in 1877, the Union Pacific Railroad constructed a station, a brick building in the High Victorian Gothic style (Figs. 85, 86). The name of the architect is not known. In plan the station follows a U shape, with the ground floor containing the station facilities, including separate waiting rooms for men and women, as was

60

customary at the time. The central part of the U rose to the second floor, and at this level and in the attic of the central pavilion of the second floor was a hotel.

Fig. 81. Clarinda. Iowa Hospital for the Insane. Architect's working drawing, 1884.

Fig. 82. Ames. Iowa State University. Morrill Hall. Early view. Courtesy Iowa State University Library, Special Collections.

Fig. 83. Cherokee. Hospital for the Insane. Main Building front, showing administration pavilion and north wing. Photo John David Langholz 1974.

Fig. 84. Cherokee. Hospital for the Insane. Detail of Main Building administration pavilion. Photo John David Langholz 1974.

Fig. 85. Council Bluffs. Union Pacific Depot. Photo J. Chris Jensen 1934.

Fig. 86. Council Bluffs. Union Pacific Depot. Photo J. Chris Jensen 1934.

At Des Moines in the early 1890s the Equitable Assurance Company Building (now Bankers Trust Building) was erected (Fig. 87). It rose eight stories in height and had been designed by the Boston architects Andrews, Jacques, and Rantoul.[30] The outer walls were of load-bearing masonry, with gray granite at the lower two floors and red brick above. The inner construction made use of an iron frame with fireproof terra cotta blocks used for the floor construction and for covering the iron frame. Three passenger elevators brought people to

Fig. 87. Des Moines. Equitable Life Assurance Company (now Bankers Trust Building). Photo Robert Thall 1977.

the offices. The building provided its own system for generating electricity; heating was by steam, although each suite of offices had a fireplace, and the owners provided the law library for the use of their tenants. The present top four floors were added in the early twentieth century. The original building is in a reserved Richardson Romanesque style, and the addition harmonizes with it.

In addition to buildings, recorded nineteenth-century structures in Iowa include two bridges, both of which have been moved from their original locations and placed in public parks. One of these bridges is now called the Owens Covered Bridge (Fig. 88). It was built near Carlisle in the later part of the century. Two eight-bay Howe trusses of wooden posts and iron rods flank the plank deck of the bridge, and wooden walls and roof protect it.[31] Many nineteenth-century covered bridges survive in Iowa. Madison County has a large number. The other recorded bridge, built in 1893, is now called the Melan Bridge, after the Austrian inventor of the system of construction used for it. It was the first reinforced-concrete highway bridge in the United States.[32]

Fig. 88. Des Moines. Owens Covered Bridge, Lake Easter Park. Photo C. C. Woodburn 1934.

EARLY TWENTIETH CENTURY

In general, the architecture of this period in Iowa was similar to that in the rest of the United States. Thus, in public buildings a Classic Revival style was frequently used, probably reflecting the influence upon the Midwest of the World's Columbian Exposition of 1893 in Chicago, which presented a strong image of a "great white city" à la imperial Rome, improved with electrical illumination. But, in addition, Chicago exerted a strong regional influence in

Iowa toward an original architecture in which the designer rejected historic antecedents and began to derive the form of his buildings mainly from the requirements of the architectural problems themselves. The architects of the late nineteenth-century skyscrapers in Chicago had led the way. In the early twentieth century an architectural philosophy was formulated in greater detail by Louis Sullivan and then Frank Lloyd Wright, and their work and that of their followers in Chicago came to be known as the Prairie style.

The Polk County Courthouse (Figs. 89, 90) is a good example in Iowa of the Classical Revival style. Erected in 1902–07 in the Courthouse Square in Des Moines, this substantial limestone structure is dominated by a central tower which surmounts a roofed courtyard surrounded by galleries and graced with impressive stairways which express the gravity of the bureaucratic and judicial activities that take place in the offices and courtrooms. The architects were the Des Moines firm of Proudfoot and Bird, who designed many public buildings in this architectural style.

Fig. 89. Des Moines. Polk County Courthouse. Photo Robert Thall 1977.

Reflecting the regional influence of Chicago toward original architecture, Chicago architects D. H. Burnham and Company designed the Fleming Building (Fig. 91) in Des Moines, which was completed in 1909. This building is an eleven-story office building with a steel frame carrying the principal loads. It has a granite cladding at the lower floors and pressed brick above. The area of windows is large and the amount of architectural ornament small. From the outside one can clearly visualize the three-dimensional grid of the steel frame.[33] The design is a notable advance over the earlier Equitable Assurance Company Building nearby, both in system of construction and in architectural expression. Similarly advanced is the John D. Van Allen and Son Dry Goods Store built in Clinton in 1913–15 (Figs. 92, 93). Louis Sullivan was the architect

Fig. 90. Des Moines. Polk County Courthouse. Interior court at fourth-floor level. Photo Robert Thall 1977.

Fig. 91. Des Moines. Fleming Building. Photo Robert Thall 1977.

of this four-story, steel-framed building, which is functionally designed for its purposes and does not recall the architectural past. The limited amount of architectural decoration that is used follows abstracted naturalistic patterns which suggest organic biological growth. Four other Sullivan buildings are found in Iowa, of which the finest is probably the Merchants' National Bank (now the Poweshiek County National Bank) built in Grinnell in 1914 (Figs. 94, 95).

Iowa has several examples of the Prairie style, in which the architects typically stressed the horizontals, recalling those of the prairie itself in the long, low, gently-pitched or flat roofs and in the grouping of windows in horizontal

Fig. 92. Clinton. John D. Van Allen & Son Store. South elevation.

bands. The color and texture of stone, brick, plaster, glass, and wood are themselves features contributing to the design, and additional decoration, if used, takes nonhistoric forms of geometric of abstract floral designs, or of geometric patterns into which plaster surfaces are subdivided by wooden strips.

The two earliest examples of the Prairie style presently known are the Sedgwick S. Brinsmaid House in Des Moines and the First Church of Christ, Scientist, in Marshalltown. The Brinsmaid House (Fig. 96) was designed by Arthur Heun, a Chicago architect who was an acquaintance of Wright's, and was built in 1901. It was a two-story house with the long horizontals of the Prairie style, but in its planning and decorative details it lacked the coherence of Wright's work. The house was razed in 1971.[34] Hugh M. G. Garden, another Chicago architect of the Prairie style, came to Marshalltown and designed the Christian Science Church there (Fig. 97), which was built in 1902-03. Its steeply pitched crossing gable roofs dramatically express the cruciform floor plan, and bold parallel bands of moldings following around the building accentuate its eave and gable lines.[35]

The work of Frank Lloyd Wright is represented in the City National Bank and the adjoining Park Inn Hotel (Fig. 98), which were built in Mason City in 1909–10 facing the south side of the town square. Although three stories high, the buildings retain a strong horizontal emphasis because of the wide overhang of their eaves. A few years later, Walter Burley Griffin, a Prairie style architect who had been closely associated with Wright, received the commission for the design of two adjoining residential subdivisions in the city, Rock Crest and Rock Glen, and for the design of several houses there as well. The land was planned so that the houses could take advantage of the view created by the creek, the bluff, and the trees and lawn at the center of the site.[36] The Arthur Rule House (Fig. 99), built in 1913, is representative of the houses in this group.

Fig. 93. Clinton. John D. Van Allen & Son Store. Terra-cotta ornament on facade. Photo Jack E. Boucher. 1977.

With walls of stuccoed terra-cotta blocks, the main part of the house is a square in plan. Broad eaves of a low-pitched hipped roof overhang the second story. Attached to the house at the first floor was a screened porch almost as a separate pavilion, in order to catch the summer breezes. Below the porch is the garage, made accessible by the downward slope of the site. Second-floor rooms were later built above the porch, changing the outline of the house, and the porch has been enclosed. Along the two streets which intersect at the corner site of the Rule House are several other Prairie style houses. Built at the same time as the Rule House on a site high above the creek at the opposite side of the subdivision, the Melson House rises up like some kind of fortification (Fig. 100). This was also one of Griffin's designs. However, in Griffin's work one must recognize that there is very likely present a contribution by his wife, Marion Mahoney Griffin, who was also a university-trained architect of considerable talent, who had also been associated with Wright, who assisted

Fig. 94. Grinnell. Merchants' National Bank (Poweshiek County National Bank). Photo Robert Thall 1977.

Fig. 95. Grinnell. Merchants' National Bank (Poweshiek County National Bank). Interior detail of banking room. Photo Robert Thall 1977.

Fig. 96. Des Moines. Brinsmaid House. Architects' presentation drawing. Courtesy of the *Chicago Architectural Annual*, 1902.

Fig. 97. Marshalltown. First Church of Christ, Scientist. Photo Robert Thall 1977.

her husband in his work, and who seems to have chosen to remain anonymous. Other Prairie style houses in the group were the work of Francis Barry Byrne.

Another Prairie style building in Iowa is the Woodbury County Courthouse (Figs. 101, 102, 103), built in 1916–18 in Sioux City. It is important as an example of the Prairie style both for the quality of the architectural design and for the size of the building. William L. Steele was the executive architect, and he associated with the firm of Purcell and Elmslie for this commission. George Elmslie, who with Steele had worked in Sullivan's office, was the designer. He evolved a logical floor plan which placed at the ground floor the large offices to which the public needed easy access. On the second floor were the courts and the rooms related to them. These two principal floors constituted the main portions of a structure which filled the lot. Above that, and covering a smaller floor area, rose a tower of six stories, housing offices and other spaces accessible by elevator. Both on the exterior and the interior of the building, extensive use was made of sculpture, bas relief, and fine colored-glass windows and skylights in which this type of glass performed the glare-reducing function for which we today use certain gray glass. In addition, there were many murals in the central glass-roofed lobby on which the main rooms of the lower portion of the building opened.[37] The Polk County Courthouse and the Woodbury County Courthouse make an interesting comparison. A decade or so apart in time, each marks a decisive step in the development of architecture in Iowa.

Because it is so modern in appearance, the James Frederic Clarke House (Fig. 104), built in 1915–16, is perhaps a fitting building for our last example. Francis Barry Byrne, the architect, had served his apprenticeship in the profession in the office of Frank Lloyd Wright. To a degree the Clarke House resembles Wright's work, as do Byrne's designs in Mason City. The colors and

Fig. 98. Mason City. City National Bank and Park Inn Hotel. Photo Robert Thall 1977.

textures of brick, wood, plaster, and glass all contribute significantly to the architectural design; and the furniture, fabrics, and a bas relief are integrated into the over-all design of the house. But here Byrne's work seems simpler than Wright's. The slab doors, the long banks of windows grouped together under broad overhanging eaves, and the attached garage are all features found in houses built fifty years later.

Fig. 99. Mason City. Rule House. Photo Robert Thall 1977.

SUMMARY

This essay has presented the historic architecture of Iowa as a tangible record of a society as it changed from pioneer conditions to those of an established pre-industrial society and then moved on into the modern industrial era. These were changes in architecture which occurred throughout the United States, of course, where during the post-Civil War period we find an increasing differentiation of building types. Thus railroad stations, office buildings, hospitals, and college buildings, for example, were developed to meet the architectural needs of the new industrial society. In Iowa as these changes were beginning, the skills of designers and builders in the state were found to be inadequate, as was the level of technology; and often buildings failed to function acceptably or to

76

be structurally sound. They had to be repaired or to have portions removed and replaced, all at unanticipated additional expense. But by the time that the period neared its completion, the competence of the people who undertook the design and construction of buildings had risen. Architects and engineers who were the product of college educational programs began to appear, along with the builders, administrators, and the effective organization required for building the new architecture and for taking advantage of such new technological developments as steel and reinforced concrete construction, electric lighting, forced-air ventilation, efficient steam heating, and electric elevators.

During this time American architects had been seeking in the architectural forms of such pre-industrial buildings as palaces, castles, Roman baths, temples, and cathedrals the inspiration for an appropriate architectural expression for the industrial era. With the beginning of the twentieth century, many middle western architects began to look for an appropriate and original architectural expression of the industrial era in the architectural forms derived from that era itself. In the work of the Chicago architects Louis Sullivan and Frank Lloyd Wright and those influenced by them, important steps toward modern architecture in the United States were taken. Their buildings in Iowa are an important part of the record of their work and of the development of the architecture of the present century.

Fig. 100. Mason City. Melson House. Photo Robert Thall 1977.

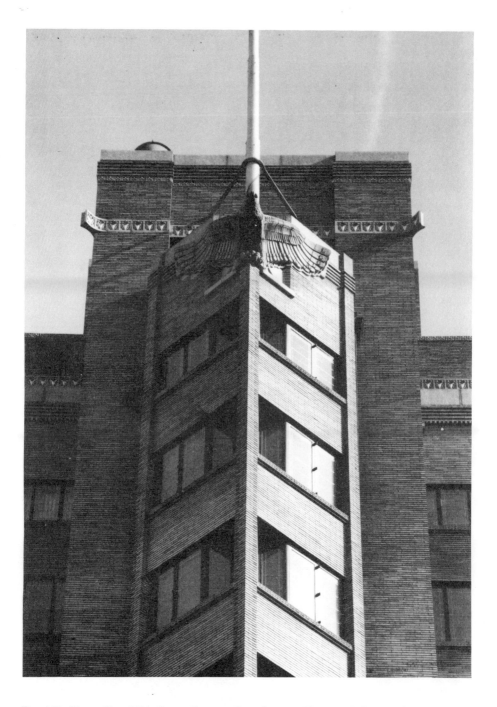

Fig. 101. Sioux City. Woodbury County Courthouse. Photo Jack E. Boucher 1976.

Fig. 102. Sioux City. Woodbury County Courthouse. Interior rotunda. Photo Jack E. Boucher 1976.

Fig. 103. Sioux City. Woodbury County Courthouse. Detail of ornamental figures over southeast entrance. Photo Jack E. Boucher 1976.

Fig. 104. Fairfield. Dr. James Frederic Clarke House. Photo Roland Wehner 1977.

NOTES

1   Robert P. Sweirenga, *Pioneers and Profits: Land Speculation on the Iowa Frontier* (Ames, Iowa: Iowa State University Press, 1968), p. 7.

2   Daniel J. Boorstin, *The Americans: The Democratic Experience* (New York: Random House, 1973), pp. 119–20. The author refers to a comment by E. V. Smalley, editor of the *Northwest Illustrated Monthly Magazine*, in 1893.

3   Leland L. Sage, *A History of Iowa* (Ames, Iowa: Iowa State University Press, 1974), pp. 107, 108.

4   Ruth Porter, "Mars Hill Log Church," *The Iowan* 20 (Fall 1971), 48, 49, 51.

5   Thomas Jefferson Wertenbaker, *The Founding of American Civilization: The Middle Colonies* (New York: Charles Scribner's Sons, 1938), pp. 303, 305.

6   Augustine M. Anthrobus, *History of Des Moines County, Iowa, and Its People* (Chicago: S. J. Clarke Publishing Co., 1915), 1:101, 102, 399.

7   Willis Edwards Parsons, *Fifty Years of Parsons College, 1875–1925* (Fairfield, Iowa: Parsons College, 1925), p. 40.

8   Johnson Brigham, *History of Des Moines and Polk County* (Chicago: S. J. Clarke Publishing Co., 1911), 2:65, 66.

9   Bertha M. H. Shambaugh, *Amana, the Community of True Inspiration* (Iowa City, Iowa: State Historical Society of Iowa, 1908), pp. 95, 140, 141, 150, 155.

10   Clair Watson, "The Amana Style in Architecture," *The Iowan* 7 (June–July), 18–22.

11   Sage, *A History of Iowa*, pp. 139, 140.

12   H. M. Hoffman, "John Francis Rague—Pioneer Architect of Iowa," *Annals of Iowa*, ser. 3, 19 (July 1933–April 1935), 444, 446.

13   Edgar Ruby Harlan, *A Narrative History of the People of Iowa* (Chicago: American Historical Society, Inc., 1931), pp. 148, 149.

14   Betsy H. Woodman, "John Francis Rague: Mid Nineteeth Century Revivalist Architect (1797–1877)" (Master's thesis, University of Iowa, 1969), pp. 6, 27, 69.

15   John E. Briggs, "Removal of the Capitol to Des Moines," *Iowa Journal of History and Politics*, 14 (1916), 91, 92, 94.

16   Woodman, "John Francis Rague," pp. 131, 133, 134, 143, 144.

17   Woodman, "John Francis Rague," pp. 152, 155, 163.

18   David J. Rothman, *The Discovery of the Asylum* (Boston: Little Brown and Co., 1971).

19   D. C. Mott, "The Quakers in Iowa," *Annals of Iowa*, ser. 3, 4 (January 1900), 265, 267, 268.

20   Museum, Amana, Iowa. Display on the West Amana Flour Mill.

21   E. T. Mix, architect. Working drawings of the William Larrabee House at the State Historical Society, Iowa City.

22   George S. Mills, *The Little Man with the Long Shadow* (Des Moines, Iowa: Trustees of the Frederick M. Hubbell Estate, 1955), pp. 171–73.

23   Genevieve P. Mauk and William J. Petersen, "Grenville Mellen Dodge, Soldier and Engineer," *Palimpsest* 47 (November 1966), 460–64.

24   Mills, *The Little Man*, p. 182.

25   Until this invention, wall plaster had consisted of lime plaster, usually applied in two thick coats, over which a hard, thin finish coat consisting of a mixture of gypsum and lime was applied. As the eventual result of the new gypsum plaster invented by Vincent and his associates, which they placed on the market in 1878, lime plaster for base coats disappeared, having been replaced by gypsum base coat plaster.

26   Orson S. Fowler, *The Octagon House: A Home for All* (New York: Dover Publications, Inc., 1973; reprint of original edition of 1853), p. 108.

27   George Shane, "Built in 1885 to Carry Out a Mother's Vow," *Des Moines Register,* June 4, 1950, p. 2L.

28   Henry-Russell Hitchcock, *Architecture: Nineteenth and Twentieth Centuries* (Baltimore: Penguin Books, 1958), pp. 191–92.

29   Paul Kenneth Goeldner, "Temples of Justice: Nineteenth Century Courthouses in the Midwest and Texas" (Ph.D. dissertation, Columbia University, 1970), pp. 237, 249.

30   *American Architect and Building News* 35 (1892), 62 and plates.

31   Leroy G. Pratt, *Discovering Historic Iowa* (Des Moines, Iowa: Department of Public Instruction, 1972), p. 171.

32   Carl W. Condit, *American Building Art: Nineteenth Century* (New York: Oxford University Press, 1960), pp. 249, 250.

33   Charles Moore, *Daniel H. Burnham, Planner of Cities* (Boston: Houghton Mifflin & Co., 1921), 2: 213.

34   Wesley I. Shank, "'The Residence in Des Moines,'" *Journal of the Society of Architectural Historians* 29 (March 1970), 58, 59.

35   Wesley I. Shank, "Hugh Garden in Iowa," *Prairie School Review* 5 (1968), 43, 44.

36   Robert E. McCoy, "Rock Crest/Rock Glen: Prairie Planning in Iowa," *Prairie School Review* 5 (1968), 15–17.

37   "Woodbury County Courthouse, Sioux City, Iowa," *Western Architect* (February 1921), 7.

BIBLIOGRAPHIC ESSAY

Little has been written about the historic architecture of Iowa. One suspects that few Iowans have been aware of it. William J. Petersen's valuable topical bibliography, *Iowa History Reference Guide* (Iowa City, Iowa: State Historical Society of Iowa, 1942) includes a section on the arts, but contains no references to articles dealing with architecture. There is also a section on business and industry, but it contains no references to the building industry. Since World War II, however, interest has begun to develop in historic architecture as more Iowans have become interested in their historical heritage. But virtually all of the material that has been written treats of selected architectural topics: the architecture of a certain locality, an architect or a builder, or a particular building. An exception was the master's thesis of William M. Dikis at Iowa State University in 1967, which was intended to lead toward a guidebook of architecture in Iowa, past and present.

Looking first at nineteenth-century architecture, we find that Margaret N. Keyes's *Nineteenth Century Home Architecture of Iowa City* (Iowa City, Iowa: University of Iowa Press, 1966) gives an accurate account of the subject undertaken and, in addition, includes a chapter about the founding of the city and its early history, and another chapter on two historic churches there. In an article entitled "He Left a Legacy in Landmarks," *The Iowan* 20 (Fall 1971), Dr. Keyes describes the homes and furniture built by Marsden Keyes in Mount Vernon, Iowa, in the late nineteenth century. Another article about the architecture of a particular city, in this case Des Moines, is Ernest E. Clark's "Architecture in Iowa's Capital City," *Midland Monthly* 10 (August–September 1898), a layman's impressions at that time. Clair Watson, with a discerning and experienced eye, deals with another locality in "The Amana Style in Architecture," *The Iowan* 7 (June–July 1959). The life of Iowa's first architect of note is briefly discussed in H. M. Hoffman's "John Francis Rague—Pioneer Architect of Iowa," *Annals of Iowa* 19 (October 1934), in which some of his buildings are mentioned. A rewarding study of Rague's work, including several floor plans, is Betsy Woodman's master's thesis at the University of Iowa (1969), "John Francis Rague: Mid Nineteenth Century Revivalist Architect (1799–1877)." Another valuable document is Paul K. Goeldner's Ph.D. dissertation done at Columbia University in 1970, "Temples of Justice: Nineteenth Century Courthouses in the Midwest and Texas," in which he studied the county courthouse as a building type, including several in Iowa. The appendix contains useful data on the architects of the courthouses studied. LeRoy Pratt's *The Counties and Courthouses of Iowa* (Mason City, Iowa: Klipto Printing and Office Supply Co., 1977) includes photographs and architectural and historical data on the state's courthouses. A curious type of building associated with county government was the subject of Walter A. Lunden's article "Rotary Jail, or Human Squirrel Cage," *Journal of the Society of Architectural Historians* 18 (December 1959).

Writing on twentieth-century architecture in Iowa is limited largely to that of the Prairie School. Robert McCoy, a resident of the subject of his article, wrote "Rock Crest/Rock Glen: Prairie Planning in Iowa," *Prairie School Review* 5 (1968), describing the work of Frank Lloyd Wright, Walter Burley Griffin, Francis Barry Byrne, and other architects in Mason City. The same issue of this magazine carries Wesley I. Shank's article, "Hugh Garden in Iowa," about the First Church of Christ, Scientist, in Marshalltown. Shank's the "'The Residence in Des Moines,'" *Journal of the Society of Architectural Historians* 29 (March 1970), deals with the S. S. Brinsmaid House in Des Moines, which, with the church, appear to be the earliest Prairie School buildings in Iowa. David Franklin Martin in his master's thesis at Iowa State University (1978), "The Moderately Priced House and the Prairie School," includes Mason City in his study. The most comprehensive treatment of the style in Iowa, however, is Richard Guy Wilson's and Sidney K. Robinson's book, *The Prairie School in Iowa* (Ames: Iowa State University Press, 1977), which examines the development of the style in the state. For the best general work on the Prairie School in the United States as a whole, the reader is referred to Harold Allen Brooks's *The Prairie School* (Toronto: University of Toronto Press, 1972).

For further information on the buildings included in "Historic Architecture in Iowa," the reader is referred to the published information cited in the footnotes and to the data pages listed in the Catalog.

Acknowledgments

In addition to the acknowledgments made elsewhere in this catalog, I wish to express my gratitude to the students of Iowa State University—many now professionals in the design and planning fields—for their interest and help over the years in identifying and recording historic buildings in the state; to my colleagues at the university for their sharing of information with me about these buildings; to Adrian Anderson, State Preservation Officer, and Richard H. Thomas, Chairperson of the Board of the State Historical Department of Iowa, for their support of publication; and especially to Nancy B. Schwartz, architectural historian with the Historic American Buildings Survey, for her care and thoroughness in the final coordination, research, and editing necessary for a finished product.

THE IOWA CATALOG

Historic American Buildings Survey

The Iowa Catalog

Agency   **Wapello County (90)**

Agency House (Old Agency House) (IA–31)
   Vicinity of Chief Wapello's Memorial Park.

Wood frame with clapboards, rectangular plan with rear ell, five-bay front, two stories with one-story ell, gable roofs. Built late 1830s; demolished early 20th century. Built for General Joseph M. Street, Indian Agent, and his family. Site of signing of 1842 treaty by which the Sac and Fox Indians ceded their Iowa lands to the U.S. 1 ext. photocopy (no date).

Agency City. See Agency   **Wapello County (90)**

Amana   **Iowa County (48)**

Amana Colonies (IA–99)
   Located along State Rtes. 220, and 149 and U.S. Rte. 6 in E central Iowa.

Seven villages on land purchased in the 1850s and 60s by the Community of True Inspiration, a German Pietist group led by Christian Metz. The villages contain buildings related to the sect's unique communal life style including communal kitchens, bakeries, mills, and barns. Amana Villages were America's most successful and long lasting religious utopian experiment. 8 ext. photos (1977†, including views of West Amana, High Amana, and South Amana). NHL (Amana Villages)

General Store Building and Offices of Amana Colonies (IA–44)
   N side State Rte. 220.

Two adjoining buildings. General Store Building (west): irregular brown ashlar, three-bay front, one-and-a-half stories, gable roof. Built 1858 (carved in gable); front porch, brick addition at rear, and remodeling after 1934. Offices of Amana Colonies (east) wood frame with clapboards, four-bay front, one-and-a-half stories, gable roof. Built mid 19th c.; remodeled and enlarged after 1934. 2 ext. photos (1934, 1977). NHL (Amana Villages)

Haas, John, House (now Ox Yoke Inn) (IA–46)
    S side State Rte. 220.

Red brick, wood frame with clapboard wings, irregular plan, four-bay front (brick portion), two-and-a-half stories, gable roofs. Built 1855 or later; remodeled and enlarged with brick and frame additions after 1934 as a restaurant. 2 ext. photos (1934, 1977). NHL (Amana Villages)

Lauer Meetinghouse (IA–18)
    In block N of State Rte. 220.

Irregular ashlar, six-bay front, one-and-a-half stories, gable roof with dormers. Built after mid 19th c.; demolished after 1934. 1 ext. photo (1934)

* *Main Meeting House* (IA–84)   (Fig. 51)
    In block N of State Rte. 220.

Irregular brown ashlar at central portion with small clapboard portions at each side, long rectangular plan, fourteen-bay central portion, one-and-a-half stories at center, two stories at ends, gable roofs. Built after mid 19th c. 1 ext. photo (1977). NHL (Amana Villages)

Mill Complex (IA–42)
    SE side of Amana.

Red brick and frame industrial structures, one-and-a-half and two stories, tall smoke stack. Complex included saw mill and woolen mill serviced by seven-mile-long power canal built in early 1860s; woolen mill still standing. Part of communal industries carried on by the Amana Colonies. 1 ext. photo (1934), 2 ext. photos of woolen mill (1977†). NHL (Amana Villages)

* *Moershal, W. F., House* (IA–47)   (Fig. 32)
    N side State Rte. 220.

Irregular brown ashlar and red brick, wings and connected outbuildings of wood frame with clapboards, stone and brick portions together comprise a rectangular plan with seven-bay front, stone part one-and-a-half stories and brick part two-and-a-half stories, frame parts one to one-and-a-half stories, gable roofs. "W M 1858" carved in gable of stone part. 2 ext. photos (1934, 1977). NHL (Amana Villages)

Offices of Amana Colonies. See General Store Building and Offices of Amana Colonies (IA–44)

Pitz Meetinghouse (IA–43)
    In block N of State Rte. 220.

Irregular brown ashlar, rectangular plan, two-bays by three-bays, one-and-a-half stories, connected to similar-sized wood-frame building at rear, gable roof, vertical sundial built into side wall. Built after mid 19th c.; converted into a residence. 1 ext. photo (1934). NHL (Amana Villages)

Amana Vicinity   **Iowa County (48)**

West Amana Flour Mill. See West Amana, West Amana Flour Mill (IA–45)

Ames   **Story County (85)**

* *Iowa State University, College Building* (Old Main) (IA–116)   (Fig. 78)
   On present site of Beardshear Hall, on Morrill Rd., facing E toward central
   campus.

Brick above rock-faced ashlar basement, E-shaped plan, 156′ (13-bay front),
three-and-a-half stories plus basement, mansard and truncated-pyramidal
roofs with dormers, originally housed all college and related functions. Built
1864–68; Charles A. Dunham, architect; wings extended 1872; assembly room-
recreation hall added 1892, Josselyn and Taylor, architects; burned 1900 and
1902; demolished. Iowa State Agricultural College opened in this building in
1868. Photocopy of drawing (ca. 1868†), 2 ext. photocopies (ca. 1870†, ca.
1897†), 1 int. photocopy (ca. 1891†); 43 data pages (1972†).

Iowa State University, Farm House (IA–123)
   40′ W of Knoll Rd., adjoining central campus.

Historic house museum. Brick with natural gray stucco, approximately 42′
(three-bay front) x 32′, with 16′ x 24′ ell at rear and 12′ x 31′ wood-frame addition at rear, two-and-a-half stories, gable roofs with dormer, entrance porch
with wooden Tuscan columns, side and rear screened porches; central hall
plan. Built 1860–65; Milens Burt, architect. Present entrance porch ca. 1895;
exterior stuccoing, side screened porch, and interior remodeling ca. 1910,
Proudfoot, Bird and Rawson, architects; garage added 1926, removed 1974;
under restoration to 1910 period, 1972–75. First building on campus. Residence
of Seaman A. Knapp, noted agriculturalist and teacher, and of James F. Wilson, U.S. Secretary of Agriculture, 1897–1913. 5 ext. photocopies (before 1896†,
ca. 1896†, 1911†, 1912–26†), 1 int. photocopy (ca. 1896†); 33 data pages (1972†);
HABSI (1967). NHL

* *Iowa State University, Morrill Hall* (IA–50)   (Fig. 82)
   On Morrill Rd., facing E toward central campus.

Red brick above rock-faced ashlar basement, 131′-8″ (front) x 63′-9″, three
stories plus basement, hipped roof with intersecting gables, four chimneys for
gravity ventilation, interior fire wall and fire doors, Richardsonian Romanesque arcade with Queen Anne style gables; contained classrooms, laboratories, museum, library, and chapel. Built 1890–91; Josselyn and Taylor, architects. Interior remodeled ca. 1913, Proudfoot, Bird and Rawson, architects. 2
ext. photocopies (undated†), 3 int. photocopies (undated†); 22 data pages
(1972†).

Arnolds Park   **Dickinson County (30)**

Gardner, Rowland, Log Cabin (Abbie Gardner Sharp Log Cabin) (IA–40)
   Monument St.

Historic house museum of the State Historical Society of Iowa. Log cabin, one story, gable roof. Built 1856; under restoration 1974–75, William J. Wagner, architect. Family home of Abbie Gardner Sharp, only survivor of Spirit Lake Massacre which occurred here in 1857. 1 ext. photocopy (no date). NR

Bentonsport   Van Buren County (89)

Bentonsport Academy (Public School Building) (IA–117)
    W side of town.

Brick on stone foundations, three bays by three bays, two stories, cupola. Built 1851 as a private academy; roof altered, cupola removed and parapet added across front. 1 ext. photocopy (no date, showing building before alteration).

* *Hancock House* (IA–19)   (Figs. 13, 14, 15, 16, 17)
    SW corner 3rd and Walnut Sts.

Wood frame with clapboards, 36'-3'' (five-bay front) x 34'-3'', two-story front, one-and-a-half story rear, gable roofs, central entrance and second-floor window both with sidelights, wood carving at entrance bay and cornice; central hall plan. Built in 1850s by James Brown. 9 sheets (1934, including plans, elevations, section, details); 4 ext. photos (1934), 1 ext. photocopy (no date); HABSI (1964). NR

Post Office (IA–48)
    Facing S on Front St.

Museum. Board-and-batten, three bays (front) by two bays, one-and-a-half stories, gable roof with decorative bargeboard, Gothic Revival details. Built mid 1840s; originally a residence. 1 ext. photo (1934); HABSI (1964).

Presbyterian Church (IA–115)
    Corner 3rd and Walnut Sts.

Red brick, one story, four-bay flank, gable roof with tower, projecting entrance vestibule with pointed-arch doorway, buttresses at corners and between bays, Gothic Revival details. Built in mid 19th c. 1 ext. photo (1934).

Boone   Boone County (8)

City Hall (IA–105)
    SE corner of 8th St. and Allen St.

Red brick, about 54' (seven-bay front) x about 48', two stories, concrete archivolts, keystones, etc., corbeled brick cornice. Built 1874–75; razed early 1970s. 1 ext. photocopy (no date†); 5 data pages (1974†); HABSI (1971).

Burlington   Des Moines County (29)

* *Carpenter, G. B. P., House* (IA–108)   (Fig. M-9)
    100 block Polk St. (Prospect Point), overlooking Mississippi River.

Stone first story, second story of wood frame filled in with brick laid flat, irregular plan, two-and-a-half stories, jerkin-head roofs, one-story verandas with simple braced columns, tall paneled chimneys, Stick style details. Built 1877; Dunham & Jordan, architects. Photocopy of sketch and plan (1879†).

First Brick House in Iowa. See Rorer, Judge David, House (IA–24)

First Masonic Building. See Remey and Webber Grocery Store (IA–118)

First Territorial Capitol. See Methodist Episcopal Church of Burlington (IA–27)

Harris House (IA–26)
   W side Main St. just S of High St.

Brick (?), rectangular with side additions, modified gable roof, two-story porch across front, exterior stairway to second floor. Built mid 19th c.; served as a tavern into the 20th c.; demolished. 1 ext. photocopy (no date).

* *Hedge Hill* (Thomas Hedge House) (IA–85)   (Fig. M-3)
   609 5th St.

Brick with wood and stone trim, rectangular, three-bay front, two-and-a-half stories on raised basement, low hipped roof, wide eaves with brackets, denticulated cornice, rinceau frieze with round windows, one-story balustraded entrance porch with paired columns, semicircular-arched doorway, corner quoins, cornice-on-consoles above windows; central hall plan, Italianate style. Built 1858. 1 ext. photo (1977†).

* *Mason, Judge Charles, House* (IA–3)   (Figs. 61, 62)
   931 N. 6th St.

Painted brick, ashlar basement, 47'-10" square plan (three-bay front) with rear ell projecting 47'-6", two-and-a-half stories, mansard roof with dormers, two entrance porches; modified central hall plan, Second Empire style. Built ca. 1866; attributed to Louis Lloyd and David Reid; converted into apartments. Mason was first chief justice of the Iowa Territory Supreme Court, under whom the Ralph case was tried in 1839. 7 sheets (1934, including plans, elevations, section, details); 3 ext. photos (1934, 1977).

Methodist Episcopal Church of Burlington (Old Zion, First Territorial Capitol) (IA–27)
   W side 3rd St., between Columbia and Washington Sts.

Brick, 40' (three-bay front) x 60', one story on stone basement, gable roof with gable end forming pediment, front bays separated by pilasters, three-stage tower with spire, Greek Revival style. Built 1838, alterations including vestibule, stairways, and adding of steeple, 1846; further alterations 1864; served as meeting place of legislature of the Territory of Iowa 1838–41, also served as courtrooms, schoolhouse, and community meeting hall; demolished 1881. 1 ext. photocopy (no date).

Old Zion. See Methodist Episcopal Church of Burlington (IA–27)

Remey and Webber Grocery Store (First Masonic Building) (IA–118)
    SE corner Main and Columbia Sts.

Frame commercial building, clapboarded, three-bay front, two stories, gable roof with gable end to street, second-story balcony. Probably built 1830s; rear additions; demolished. During 1838, the House of Representatives of the Assembly of the Territory of Wisconsin met in second-floor meeting rooms; the first Masonic lodge in the state (chartered 1841) met there also. 1 ext. photocopy (no date).

* *Rorer, Judge David, House* (First Brick House in Iowa) (IA–24)   (Fig. 10)
    SE corner N. 4th St. and Columbia.

Brick, four-bay front, one story above basement, gable roof with stepped gable-end walls. Built 1836; demolished before 1915. Said to be first brick house in Iowa. 1 ext. photocopy (no date).

Carlisle Vicinity   Polk County (77)

Covered Bridge (Owens Covered Bridge) (IA–2)
    Originally crossed old channel of North River, approx. 2 mi. NE of Carlisle, sec. 35, Allen Twp., Polk Co. Moved to Lake Easter Park, entrance at 2830 SE. 52nd Ave.

Board-and-batten walls, timber-and-iron eight-bay Howe trusses, plank deck, shingled gable roof. Built late 19th c. Moved in late 1960s from original Polk County site NE of Carlisle in the Red Rock Reservoir area. 4 sheets (1934, including plans, elevations, architectural and structural details); 2 ext. photos (1934).

Cedar Rapids   Linn County (57)

* *Hamilton, James E., House* (IA–86)   (Fig. M-15)
    2345 Linden Ave., SE.

Stuccoed concrete block walls, two stories, tiled gable roof, tall exterior end chimney with tile cap, projecting entrance pavilion, compound pointed-arch doorway, three round-arched casement windows above, decorative iron grillework, Mediterranean style details. Built 1929–30; Ernest Kennedy of Minneapolis, architect; interior plasterwork and ceiling mural attributed to Grant Wood. Hamilton was founder of Merchants National Bank. 1 ext. photo (1977).

Cherokee   Cherokee County (18)

Hospital for the Insane (now called State Mental Health Institute at Cherokee), Main Building (IA–51)   (Figs. 83, 84)
    At NW edge of town, N of W. Main St.

Red brick and yellowish brick above coursed, rock-cut reddish jasper foundation, echelon plan about 970' wide by about 330' deep consisting of two units on a central axis and three connected units symmetrically placed on each side, two-and-a-half, three-and-a-half, and four-and-a-half stories, hipped roofs with dormers and louvered cupolas, whitish rock-cut stone string courses, round and polygonal bay-window towers, central hall plan in each unit, Queen Anne style. Built 1896–1902; Josselyn and Taylor, architects until 1897; Henry F. Liebbe after. 5 ext. photos (1974†), 2 photocopies of original drawings (no date†); 31 data pages (1974†).

Clarinda   Page County (73)

* *Iowa Hospital for the Insane* (now called State Mental Health Institute at Clarinda), Main Building (IA–52)   (Fig. 81)
   W side of 12th St., N of town.

Red brick with gray stone string courses, modified echelon plan about 1150' wide by about 390' deep consisting of two units on a central axis and three connected units symmetrically placed on each side, two-and-a-half and three stories, hipped roofs and mansard roof with dormers at center, cupolas, central five-story tower, central hall plan in each unit, Eastlake style. Built 1884–99; Foster and Liebbe, architects. 3 ext. photos (1974†), 3 int. photocopies (ca. 1895†), 3 photocopies of original drawings (ca. 1884†); 39 data pages (1974†).

Clermont Vicinity   Fayette County (33)

* *Montauk* (Gov. William Larrabee House) (IA–66)   (Figs. 56, 57)
   U.S. Rte. 18, one mi. NE of Clermont.

Historic house museum. Red brick with dolomite foundation, window hoods and sills, 40' (three-bay front) x 60' (three bays), two-and-a-half stories, hipped roof with balustraded deck, bracketed wooden cornice, attic windows in frieze, projecting entrance pavilion with one-story wooden columnar porch, walls articulated by pilasters, Italianate style, original outbuildings. Built 1874; Edward Townsend Mix, architect. William Larrabee was governor of Iowa 1886-94 and a nationally prominent crusader against railroad rate abuses. House and furnishings unchanged since Larrabee's residence. 2 ext. photos (1977), 3 int. photos (1977); HABSI (1970). NR

Clinton   Clinton County (23)

* *Clinton County Courthouse* (IA–100)   (Figs. 75, 76)
   In Courthouse Square, bounded by N. 2nd and N. 3rd Sts. and by 6th and 7th Aves. North.

Rock-faced ashlar of reddish-brown color, three-and-a-half stories, hipped roof with gables at projecting bays, dormers, central tower sheathed in copper embossed to resemble rock-faced ashlar, square plan with full-height cylindrical towers at corners, Richardsonian Romanesque style. Built 1892–97; G. Stanley Mansfield, architect. 3 ext. photos (1977†), 3 int. photos (1977†); HABSI (1968).

U.S. Post Office (IA–112)
  SW corner of 5th Ave. S. and S. 3rd St.

Rusticated limestone ashlar, five bays (front) x three bays, one story, balustraded eaves, screen of four engaged Ionic columns across front, flat-and-round-arched fenestration with scroll keystones and false balustrades, Classical Revival style. Built 1904; James Knox Taylor, Supervising Architect of the Treasury. 3 ext. photos (1977†).

*Van Allen, John D., and Son Store (now Petersen Harned Von Mauer Store)
  (IA–22)   (Figs. 92, 93)
  NW corner 5th Ave. S. and S. 2nd St.

Steel-frame structural system, yellow-gray brick veneer with verd antique marble and terra cotta trim, 86′ (three-bay front) x 90′ with rear wing, four stories, flat roof, terra cotta ornament. Built 1913–15. Louis H. Sullivan, architect; fine example of his late work. 8 sheets (1960s, including plot plan, plans, elevations, details); 4 ext. photos (1977†); HABSI (1962). NHL

Council Bluffs   Pottawattamie County (78)

* Dodge, Gen. Grenville M., House (IA–5)   (Figs. 59, 60)
  605 S. 3rd St.

Historic house museum. Brick, excluding porch, 54′-4″ (four-bay front) x 53′, two-and-a-half stories, mansard roof with dormers, large veranda; central hall plan, Second Empire style. Built 1869; W. W. Boyington, architect; many additions and alterations; restored in 1960s. Dodge was chief engineer of transcontinental Union Pacific Railroad. 3 sheets (1934, including plans, interior elevations and details); 5 ext. photos (after 1916, 1977), 5 int. photos (after 1916); 8 data pages (1961, 1963). NHL

*Iowa Institution for the Education of the Deaf and Dumb (now Iowa State School
  for the Deaf), Main Building (IA–53)   (Fig. 79)
  E of intersection of South Ave. and State Rte. 92.

Brick above rock-faced ashlar basement, 23-bay front, four stories at center, three stories at each side, all above basement, gable roofs, central tower. Built in phases, 1868–80; Schwarz and Dilger, architects; destroyed by fire, 1902. A. J. Davis submitted a preliminary design, not followed. 2 ext. photocopies (ca. 1887†, no date†); 17 data pages (1972†).

Pottawattamie County Courthouse (IA–87)
  NW Corner Pearl St. and 5th Ave.

Limestone, five-part with projecting three-story central and end pavilions and two-story links, raised basement, hipped and gable roofs, mansards with elaborate dormers over corner pavilions, pediments centered over central and side entrances, top floors articulated with paired pilasters, Second Empire and Renaissance Revival details. Built 1885–88; Eckel and Mann, architects. To be demolished for parking lot. 3 ext. photos (1977), 1 int. photo (1977).

Pottawattamie County Jail (IA–88)
   226 Pearl St., N of county courthouse.

Brick with limestone trim, two-and-a-half stories, gable and hipped roofs, wall dormers, bracketed and corbeled cornices, High Victorian Gothic details; front portion with cross-gable roof was jailer's residence; octagonal rear section with hipped roof and cupola contains three circular tiers of jail cells which rotate within a steel cage. Built 1885; Eckel and Mann, architects; rotary cell design patented by W. H. Brown; cells supplied by Haugh, Ketcham Co. of Indianapolis. 2 ext. photos (1977†). NR

* *Sutherland, Mrs. D. B., House* (IA–103)   (Fig. M-11)

Frame with shingle covering, asymmetrical plan, two-and-a-half stories, steep gable roof with semihexagonal corner turret, decorative dormer with balcony, roof sweeps out to cover front porch, exposed rafter ends, Shingle style. Built ca. 1891; J. Hackett Kent, architect. Photocopy of sketch (1892†).

* *Union Pacific Depot* (Transfer Depot and Hotel) (IA–6)   (Figs. 85, 86, M-5)
   21st St., two blocks S of 9th Ave.

Brick, U-shaped plan, 210'-5" (19-bay front) x 221'-3", at center two-and-a-half stories with dormers, sides two stories, ells one story, mansard roofs with gable roofs at ells, High Victorian Gothic style; ground floor contained station facilities, second floor and attic were hotel rooms. Built 1877; demolished. 10 sheets (1934, including plans, elevations, sections, details); 6 ext. photos (1934).

Davenport   **Scott County (82)**

* *Grace Episcopal Cathedral* (now Trinity Episcopal Cathedral) (IA–114)
   1121 Main St.   (Figs. 70, 71)

Rock-faced broken yellowish ashlar limestone, 82' (three-bay front) x 135' (four bays plus apse), one story, gable roof, small dormers, clerestory strip, iron filigree ridge cresting; basilican plan, laminated-wood nave trusses, Gothic Revival style. Built 1867–73; Edward Tuckerman Potter, architect; parish house added 1917. 5 ext. photos (1977†), 4 int. photos (1977†); 12 data pages (1972†). NR

* *Parker, J. Monroe, House* (Ficke Mansion) (IA–113)   (Figs. M-6, M-7)
   NW corner Main and 12th Sts.

Brick with limestone, pressed metal and wooden trim, asymmetrical plan, two stories with third story under patterned slate mansard roof, three-story projecting entrance tower, numerous projecting bays with dormered mansard caps, cast-iron roof cresting, bracketed cornice, one-story porches, Second Empire style. Built 1881–84; Victor Huot, architect. 10 ext. photos (1977†), 4 int. photos (1977†).

* *Bucknell, W. S., House* (IA–4)   (Fig. 24)
   210–13 Winnebago St.

Stucco on limestone concrete, 30'-6'' (three-bay front) x 36'-9'' main block
with porches along front and sides, central rear ell projects 16'-2'', three-story
main block, two-story ell, one-story porch, truncated-hipped and hipped
roofs, stucco scored like stonework; divided into three living units. Reputedly
built 1855 by David Reed; side porches removed, front porch modified, exterior stairways modified, scrollwork decoration removed; re-stuccoed without scoring. 5 sheets (1934, including plans, elevations, details); 2 ext. photos
(1934).

* *City Stone Mill* (Painter-Bernatz Mill) (IA–11)   (Fig. 54)
   Mill St. at Heivly St.

Exhibition building for the Norwegian-American Museum. Limestone rubble,
wood frame with drop siding above eaves line, wood frame and clapboard
turbine house, 52'-1'' (four-bay front) x 59'-4'', with turbine house projecting
15'-1'' at side, two stories with basement and loft lighted by clerestory,
turbine house one story, gable roof above clerestory flanked by single-slope
roofs. Built 1851–53 by W. S. Painter; operated by water power until 1947;
interior floor levels and roof altered; mill machinery removed 1963; restored
ca. 1970 to 1900–14 period. 3 sheets (1934, including plans, elevations, details); 2 ext. photos (1934). NR

Des Moines   **Polk County (77)**

Allen-Hubbell House. See Terrace Hill (IA–69)

Bankers Trust Building. See Equitable Life Assurance Company (IA–68)

* *Brinsmaid, S. S., House* (IA–67)   (Fig. 96)
   NE corner Grand Ave. and 36th St.

Stucco over wood frame, brown brick veneer base, approximately 40' x 60',
two stories, gable roofs with wide overhang turned up at gables, horizontal
wooden bands joining second-floor windows; irregular plan, interior stained
leaded-glass French doors and lighting fixtures, early Prairie style. Built 1901;
Arthur A. Heun of Chicago, architect; demolished 1971. Earliest known
Prairie style house in Iowa. 3 ext. photocopies (early 20th c.), 1 int. photocopy
(early 20th c.), 1 photocopy of presentation drawing (ca. 1901), photocopy of
floor plan (ca. 1970).

* *Butler, Earl, House* (now Open Bible College·) (IA–89)   (Fig. M-18)
   2633 S. Fleur Dr.

Reinforced concrete exterior walls, two and three stories on sloping site, flat
roofs, large windows, cantilevered balconies, terraced landscaping, combines
curved and rectilinear forms, streamlined house in the Moderne style of the

1930s; stark undecorated interiors, central ramp joining floors, originally had such conveniences as air conditioning, intercom system, dishwasher and disposal. Built 1935–37; Kraetsch & Kraetsch, architects. 1 ext. photo (1977).

Capitol, Temporary (Second State Capitol) (IA–30)
  Site of Soldiers and Sailors Monument S of present Capitol.

Brick, 100' (seven-bay front) x 56', three stories, flat or low-pitched roof, Italianate style. Built 1856–57 by Willson A. Scott, John Hyde, and John Bryan, contractors; demolished 1892. Occupied as capitol 1857–86. 1 ext. photocopy (no date).

* *Covered Bridge* (Owens Covered Bridge)   (Fig. 88)
  Lake Easter Park, entrance at 2830 SE. 52nd Ave. See Covered Bridge (IA–2), Carlisle Vicinity.

* *Equitable Life Assurance Company* (now Bankers Trust Building) (IA–68)
  NW corner Locust and 6th Sts.   (Fig. 87)

Cast-iron and steel frame structure, first two floors faced with gray granite, remaining ten floors are red brick with red terra cotta trim, 132' (nine-bay front) x 66' (five bays), flat roof with projecting cornice of acanthus brackets, intermediate decorative cornices, arched and rectangular windows, arcade of engaged three-story columns terminates above seventh floor, Romanesque Revival details. Built 1891 as a speculative office building; Andrews, Jacques, and Rantoul of Boston, architects; top four floors added 1911, Proudfoot, Bird, and Rawson, architects; interior alterations. 2 ext. photos (1977). NR

Federal Building, Old. See U.S. Courthouse and Post Office (IA–36)

First House in Fort Des Moines (IA–34)

Log cabin with board-and-batten addition, rectangular plan, one story, gable roof. Built 1840s; demolished. 1 ext. photocopy (ca. 1910).

First Post Office Building (IA–35)

Wood frame with clapboards, rectangular plan, one story, gable roof. Built ca. 1850 by Hoyt Sherman, postmaster; demolished. 1 ext. photocopy (no date).

* *Fleming Building* (IA–90)   (Fig. 91)
  SW corner of Walnut and 6th Sts.

Steel structural frame, polished brown granite veneer at first and second stories, brownish hydraulic pressed brick above, 132' (seven-bay front) x 68', eleven stories, flat roof, Chicago style. Completed 1909; D. H. Burnham and Company, architects. 1 ext. photo (1977).

Governor's Mansion. See Terrace Hill (IA–69)

Governor's Mansion, Old. See W. W. Witmer House (IA–104)

Granger, Barlow, House (IA–15)
   Pioneer Park

Stuccoed brick, irregular plan, 36'-9" x 66'-10", one-and-a-half stories, gable roof with dormers. First portion built 1856; demolished 1937. Granger was a pioneer newspaperman, businessman, attorney, and Democratic politician in Des Moines. 10 sheets (1934, including plans, elevations, details); 5 ext. photos (1934), 1 ext. photocopy (ca. 1900).

House (IA–91)
   1506 Thompson Ave.

Frame on raised brick foundation, narrow siding with corner boards, one-and-a-half stories, gable roof with gable end toward street, projecting enclosed entrance porch with gable roof, wide eaves with straight brackets, Bungalow style. Built ca. 1920. 1 ext. photo (1977).

Iowa Girls Highschool Athletic Association. See W. W. Witmer House (IA–104)

Open Bible College. See Earl Butler House (IA–89)

* *Polk County Courthouse* (IA–93)   (Figs. 89, 90)
   5th and Court Sts., in Courthouse Square.

Light grayish-tan limestone ashlar, lower two stories rusticated, seventeen-bay front and rear, eleven bay sides, four stories, flat roof, central staged tower in same stone, roofed central gallery plan, Classical Revival style. Built 1902–07; Proudfoot and Bird, architects. 1 ext. photo (1977); 4 int. photos (1977).

* *Rollins, Ralph, House* (IA–92)   (Fig. M-13)
   2801 S. Fleur Dr.

Brick with stone, wood and stucco trim, decorative brick bonding including diaperwork, simulated half-timbering, irregular plan giving the appearance of several additions, slate gable and hipped roofs, picturesque roofline with large dormers and chimneys, Tudor style. Built 1925; Boyd and Moore, architects. 1 ext. photo (1977).

Sakulin, Barney, Log House (IA–106)
   In Des Moines Birthplace Park, SW corner SW. First St. and Elm St.; moved from original location in Washington County.

Museum of the Polk County Historical Society. Log with stone foundation, 20'-4" (three-bay front) x 18'-3", one story, gable roof, one exterior end chimney (not original). Built ca. 1843–46; moved and reconstructed 1965; William J. Wagner, architect. 8 sheets (1965†, including site map, plans, elevations, section).

Second State Capitol. See Capitol, Temporary (IA–30)

* *Terrace Hill* (Allen-Hubbell House, now Governor's Mansion) (IA–69)
  2300 Grand Ave. (Fig. 58)

Brick with wooden trim and precast concrete quoins and window hoods, two stories with full third story under slate mansard roof, bracketed cornice, decorative dormers, wooden porch, four-stage mansarded entrance tower, three-stage secondary tower; asymmetrical central hall plan, elaborate interior hardwood trim, large stained glass window on stair landing, one of the grandest Second Empire style houses in state. Built 1867–69; W. W. Boyington of Chicago, architect; landscape design by Job T. Elletson; remodeled 1924; under restoration as governor's mansion beginning 1974. First owner was millionaire B. F. Allen who lost the house through bankruptcy in 1874; purchased in 1884 by wealthy businessman F. M. Hubbell. In Hubbell family until acquired by State of Iowa in 1971. 1 ext. photo (1977); HABSI forms (no date, 1967). NR

* *U.S. Courthouse and Post Office* (Old Federal Building) (IA–36) (Fig. 77)
  NE corner 5th St. and Court Ave.

Joliet limestone ashlar, approximately 120' square (nine-bay front), three-and-a-half stories, mansard roof with raised central pavilion, tower of pressed metal; interior three-story skylighted court, Second Empire style. Built 1867–71 as a two-and-a-half story building; Alfred B. Mullett, Supervising Architect of the Treasury; completed 1885–90; Mifflin E. Bell, architect; demolished 1968. 4 ext. photos (1968, one showing demolition†), 6 int. photos (1968†), photocopy of ca. 1871 view†; 17 data pages (1974†).

Witmer, W. W., House (Old Governor's Mansion, now Iowa Girls Highschool Athletic Association) (IA–104) (Fig. M-14)
  2900 Grand Ave.

Red brick with wooden trim, six-bay front, two-and-a-half stories, gable roof with pedimented dormers, Ionic pilasters, central pedimented pavilion with fanlighted entrance and Palladian window, semicircular entrance porch, rectangular side porch, both porches are one-story with Ionic columns and balustrades, broken pediments above first floor front windows, Georgian Revival style. Built 1905; Liebbe, Nourse and Rasmussen, architects. Served as governor's mansion from 1949 to 1976. 1 ext. photocopy (1906).

Dow City   **Crawford County (24)**

* *Dow, Simeon E., House* (IA–70) (Fig. 64)
  S end of Prince St.

Historic house museum. Red brick, irregular shape, three-bay front, two stories, hipped roof, elaborate bracketed cornice with arch above central front bay, segmental window and door lintels with label moldings, one story wooden porch across front with decorative brackets and balustrade, Italianate details. Built 1872–74 by Simeon Dow, local entrepreneur and cofounder of Dow City in 1869; restored 1971–74; Harold Hoskins and Associates, architects. 2 ext. photos (1977). NR

Archbishop's Residence. See F. D. Stout House (IA–110)

*City Hall (IA–71)   (Fig. 41)
    50 W. 13th St., between Central Ave. and Iowa St.

Red brick, structural system of cast-iron beams and columns above limestone ashlar basement, 50' (four-bay E front) x 152' (15 bays), three stories, gable roof, originally had ornate bell tower at E end, facades articulated by shallow, segmental arcades; first floor originally contained city market (one stall per bay), second floor had meeting rooms and offices, third floor was ballroom. Built 1857–58; John Francis Rague, architect; first floor subdivided for offices, bell tower removed. A rare surviving American example of the combination market and city hall, a building type which dates back to the Middle Ages. 3 ext. photos (1977†), 3 int. photos (1977†); HABSI (1969). NR

Dubuque County Courthouse (IA–109)
    720 Central Ave., NE corner Central Ave. and E. 7th St.

Red brick with gray Bedford limestone and terra cotta trim, rectangular with projecting central and corner pavilions, three-and-a-half stories on raised basement, steep slate hipped roof with gables over central pavilions, 190' central tower with octagonal cupola, galvanized metal cornice, rusticated limestone pilasters with terra cotta caps, pewter allegorical figures above main entrance and corner pavilions, Renaissance Revival with Romanesque details. Built 1891–93; Fridolin Heer & Son, architects. 7 ext. photos (1977†), 1 int. photo (1977†); HABSI (no date). NR

* Dubuque County Jail (IA–72)   (Figs. 42, 43)
    36 E. 8th St., N of the county courthouse

Limestone ashlar with cast-iron and wooden trim, L-shaped, 46'-square two-story front unit contains jailer's residence and Sheriff's office, rear wing (36' x 54') has three tiers of cells and exercise yard along W side, cast-iron cavetto lintels and jambs with winged-disk motif, main entrance flanked by cast-iron lotus columns *in antis,* wooden cavetto cornice. Built 1857–58; John Francis Rague, architect. An unusual example of the Egyptian Revival style in America. 6 ext. photos (1977†), 4 int. photos (1977†); HABSI (1967). NR

Dubuque, Julien, Monument (Grave) (IA–9)
    S of city, 3/4 mi. from end of Julien Dubuque Dr. in Julien Dubuque County Park.

Rock-faced limestone ashlar, cylindrical tower, 12'-8" diameter, two stories, unroofed, crenelated. Built 1897; remains of founder of Dubuque reinterred within. On the site before 1897 were Dubuque's original grave and graves of three Indians, thought to be his wife Potosa, his father-in-law Peosta, and his friend Kettlechief. 1 sheet (1934, including plans, elevation, section, details); 3 ext. photos (1934, 1977†).

Egelhof-Casper Funeral Home. See Fannie Stout House (IA–111)

First Church in Iowa. See Methodist Chapel (IA–39)

Five Flags Theater. See Majestic Theater (IA–124)

* *Ham, Mathias, House* (IA–73)   (Fig. M-4)
  2241 Lincoln Ave.

Museum of Dubuque City Park Board and Dubuque County Historical Society. Smooth-faced limestone ashlar with wooden trim, 45' x 73', square (three-bays per side) with rear ell, two-and-a-half stories, cross-gable roof with dormers in valleys, octagonal cupola, wide bracketed cornice, one-story entrance porch and side veranda with Tudor arches, paired windows. Built 1857; ell is original house on site, built 1839. Both erected by Dubuque businessman Mathias Ham. 11 ext. photos (1977†), 7 int. photos (1977†). NR

* *Langworthy, Edward, House* (IA–14)   (Figs. 37, 38, 39)
  1095 W. 3rd St.

Red brick, octagonal, 47'-7" across, rear ell projects 31'-2", two stories with octagonal cupola, hipped roofs, one-story bay windows with wrought-iron cresting, entrance recessed under two-story octagonal porch; central hall plan. Built late 1850s; John Francis Rague, architect; interior altered; one-story addition at NW angle in 1946. 6 sheets (1934, including plans, elevations, details); 7 ext. photos (1934, 1977†), 5 int. photos (1934, 1977†). NR

Majestic Theater (later Orpheum Theater, now Five Flags Theater) (IA–124)
  405 Main St.

Brick with limestone trim, three-bay front, convex mansard and flat roofs, rusticated ground floor and pilasters, prominent stone belt course supporting light standards, large round-arch entrance, bracketed cornice, central mansard pavilion, elaborate dormers with balcony-parapet; proscenium stage, 1000-seat auditorium with mezzanine boxes, balcony, and gallery with original wooden benches, rich interior plaster decoration, French Renaissance Revival style. Built 1910; oldest known theater by renowned Chicago firm of Rapp and Rapp. Originally a music hall and vaudeville house; converted to movie house in 1929; restored as city's bicentennial project, 1974–76, Culten, Kilby, Carolan and Assoc., architects. 3 ext. photos (1977†), 9 int. photos (1977†). NR

Methodist Chapel (First Church in Iowa) (IA–39)

Log, 20' x 26' one story, gable roof; one-room plan. Built 1834; moved and used as a dwelling before Civil War; demolished mid 19th c. Photocopy of old sketch (no date).

Orpheum Theater. See Majestic Theater (IA–124)

* *Shot Tower* (IA–8)   (Figs. 52, 53)
  Commercial St. near E end of E. 4th St.

101

Limestone rubble in irregular courses at lower six stories, red brick at upper three stories, 19'-2" square at base, 150' tall, battered walls. Built 1856 by C. H. Rogers & Co.; restored 1961. Molten lead was poured from top, through screens, into water at bottom to form lead shot for guns. 1 sheet (1934, including plans, elevation, details); 4 ext. photos (1934, 1977†); HABSI (no date). NR

* *Stout, F. D., House* (Archbishop's Residence) (IA–110)   (Fig. M-8)
   1105 Locust St.

Rusticated red sandstone, random ashlar, rectangular with projecting bays and porches, two-and-a-half stories, modified gable slate roof, three-story polygonal corner tower, Richardsonian Romanesque style, rear courtyard enclosed by attached stable; interior elaborately finished with rosewood and mahogany woodwork, screens of onyx columns separate principal rooms. Built 1890–91. The Stouts had extensive lumber interests in the West and Wisconsin; house acquired by archdiocese of Dubuque in 1911. 8 ext. photos (1977†).

* *Stout, Fannie, House* (Egelhof-Casper Funeral Home) (IA–111)   (Fig. M-10)
   1145 Locust St.

Clapboarded wooden frame with sandstone, brick, and terra cotta trim, two-and-a-half stories, hipped slate roof, circular corner tower with Moorish arcade and onion dome, projecting first- and second-story porches with floral plasterwork friezes, dormers with porches, tall sandstone chimneys, Queen Anne style. Built 1892; Fridolin Heer, architect. 6 ext. photos (1977†), 8 int. photos (1977†).

Elkader   **Clayton County (22)**

Water Mill, Turkey River (IA–37)
   E side of N. Main St., between Bridge and Cedar Sts.

Coursed limestone rubble, four bays at rear, four-and-a-half stories, gable roof, gristmill. Built early 1860s for John Thompson and Timothy Davis, replacing earlier mill on same site built in late 1840s for Thompson, Davis, and Chester Sage, founders of the town. Upper two-and-a-half stories demolished and remaining lower portion built into present adjoining commercial structures. 1 ext. photocopy (ca. 1900).

Fairfield   **Jefferson County (51)**

* *Clarke, James Frederic, House* (IA–23)   (Fig. 104)
   500 Main St., at SW corner of W. Madison

Red brick, irregular plan fitting within a rectangle 48'-6" x 72', two stories, gable roofs, Prairie style. Built 1915–16; Francis Barry Bryne, architect; Alfonso Ianelli, collaborating artist. Fine example of its style. 4 sheets (1970, including site plan, plans, elevations, section); 1 ext. photo (1977†); 15 data pages (1972†).

Henn, Bernhart, House (Parsons College, Ewing Hall; now Maharishi International University) (IA–123) (Fig. M-2)

Red brick, five-bay front with ell at rear, two-and-a-half stories with two-story ell, hipped roof with central cupola at main block, stone lintels, recessed wooden Doric columns flanking door; central hall plan. Built 1857–58 as a house for Bernhart Henn; has had several different front porches; interior remodelings. Parsons College opened in building in 1875. 1 ext. photo (1934).

Festina **Winneshiek County (96)**
* *Saint Anthony's Chapel* (IA–12) (Fig. 69)
.5 mi. SE of Festina.

Limestone rubble, 14' (one-bay front) x 20', 5'-square central tower of wood frame with drop siding, one story, gable roof and octagonal spire, barrel-vaulted wooden ceiling. Built 1885; attributed to John Gartner. 2 sheets (1934, including plan, elevations, details); 1 ext. photocopy (ca. 1900).

Floris Vicinity **Wapello County (90)**

* *Mars Hill Baptist Church* (IA–74) (Figs. 6, 7)
On unnumbered county Rte., .5 mi. S of Little Soap Creek, approx. 4 mi. NW of Floris.

Museum. Hewn logs with dovetail notching, 26' x 28', one story, gable roof with clapboarded gable ends, side windows, door in gable end, open plan. Built ca. 1850. Thought to be one of oldest log churches remaining in state. Picturesque adjacent cemetery. 1 ext. photo (1977), 2 int. photos (1977); HABSI (1956). NR

Fort Dodge **Webster County (94)**

* *Butler, J. B., House* (IA–75) (Fig. M-12)
327 S. 12th St.

Brownish Roman brick with wooden trim, two-and-a-half stories, hipped roof with dormers, one story porch with brick piers across front, porte cochere on side, broad eaves on house, porch and porte cochere show Prairie style influence, decorative work around windows and on porch piers reminiscent of Louis Sullivan. Built 1903; Nourse and Rasmussen of Des Moines, architects. Butler was a Fort Dodge lawyer and businessman. 1 ext. photo (1977). NR (Oak Hill Historic District)

* *Swain-Vincent House* (IA–38) (Fig. 63)
824 3rd Ave. South

Historic house museum of the Y.W.C.A. Red brick, 36'-9'' (three-bay front) x 66'-9'', two-and-a-half stories, mansard roof with dormers, one-story wooden veranda; side hall plan, Second Empire style. Built 1871; kitchen wing built 1901. Home of Webb Vincent, who with associates developed gypsum basecoat plaster. Gypsum plaster was first used on walls of third-floor ballroom in this house. 1 ext. photo (1977†); 14 data pages (1972†). NR

Fort Madison   **Lee County (56)**

* *Lee County Courthouse* (IA–76)   (Fig. M-1)
  701 Avenue F

Brick, 50′ (three-bay front) x 100′ (four bays), two stories, gable roof, temple plan with tetrastyle portico of brick Doric columns, entablature on all facades; central hall plan, courtroom at S end of second floor. Built 1841–42; post Civil War cupola destroyed by fire in 1911; rear additions; extensive interior alterations. One of finest Greek Revival buildings in state and one of oldest surviving courthouses. 1 ext. photo (1977). NR

Gilbert Vicinity   **Story County (85)**

Methodist Episcopal Church of Milford Township (now called Pleasant Grove Community Church) (IA–119)   (Fig. 67)
  N side of County Rd. E-23, four mi. E of Gilbert and just W of Interstate 35.

Wood frame with clapboards, concrete-block foundation, about 25′ (two-bay front) x about 40′, one story plus cellar, gable roof. Built 1873 or 1874; cellar and new foundations 1941. Typical rural church. 2 ext. photos (1972†, 1974†), 2 int. photos (1974†); 12 data pages (1974†).

Grinnell   **Poweshiek County (79)**

* *Merchants' National Bank* (Poweshiek County National Bank) (IA–77)
  NW corner Fourth Ave. and Broad St.   (Figs. 94, 95)

Wire-cut shale brick of varying shades of red, tan terra cotta ornament, 41′ x 76′, one story, flat roof, red terra cotta cornice with projecting finials, large (15′ x 40′) ten-section window on E side, circular window with exuberant terra cotta surround above main entrance on S; colorful interior stained glass windows and skylight, gilt terra cotta ornament, original hanging light fixtures. Built 1914; Louis Sullivan, architect. One of the three best preserved of the small midwestern banks built by Sullivan. 3 ext. photos (1977), 1 int. photo (1977); HABSI (1967). NHL

Hampton   **Franklin County (35)**

Franklin County Courthouse (Second) (IA–120)
  Courthouse Square, bounded by First Ave., NW.; Central Ave., N.; First St., NW.; and Federal St., N.

Coursed limestone ashlar, 40′ (three-bay front) x 70′, two stories, gable roof with gable expressed as a pediment; central hall plan first floor, Greek Revival style. Built 1866–67; Usiah Weeks, builder; demolished 1890; replaced by present courthouse. 1 ext. photocopy (before 1890†); 7 data pages (1972†).

Holy Cross   **Dubuque County (31)**

* *Western Hotel* (Pin Oak Tavern) (IA–10)   (Figs. 18, 19, 20)
S side of U.S. Rte. 52, .8 mi. E of intersection with southern extension of the
main street of Holy Cross.

Frame with clapboards, rubble-stone basement fully exposed in rear, 37'-3''
(six-bay front) x 34'-5'', one-and-a-half stories with basement rooms, gable
roof with long rear slope, porch across front. Built ca. 1850; John H. Floyd,
original owner; asbestos shingles now on walls. 2 sheets (1934, including
plans, elevations, details); 1 ext. photo (1934). NR

Independence   **Buchanan County (10)**

**Iowa Hospital for the Insane* (now State Mental Health Institute at Indepen-
dence), Main Building (IA–54)   (Fig. 80)
State Rte. 248, .5 mi. S of U.S. Rte. 20.

Coursed light gray to brown magnesian limestone with rock-cut foundation
and rusticated first floor, echelon plan consisting of three units on a central
axis and three parts to each of two wings flanking central units, four and three
stories, mansard and gable roofs with dormers; central hall plan at each unit,
Second Empire style. Built 1868–84; Stephen V. Shipman, architect. Second
state mental hospital in Iowa. 2 ext. photos (1974†), photocopy of floor plan
(ca. 1891†), photocopy of engraving (ca. 1891†); 15 data pages (1974†).

Iowa City   **Johnson County (52)**

Capitol. See Old Capitol (IA–29)

Capitol, Temporary (Second Territorial Capitol) (IA–28)

Wood frame and clapboard, nine-bay front, two stories with one-story ell
(ells?) at rear, gable roofs, pilasters and entablature at first floor. Built 1841 for
Walter Butler; demolished. First meeting place of the Territorial Legislature in
Iowa City, 1841. Served as second territorial capitol. 1 ext. photocopy (no
date).

* *Old Capitol* (Third Territorial and First State Capitol) (IA–29)   (Fig. 40)
Clinton St. and Iowa Ave.

Museum. Coursed limestone ashlar, 120' (nine-bay front) x 60', two stories
with wooden central cupola, wooden porticoes on long sides; central hall plan
with suspended spiral staircase, Greek Revival style. Built 1840–50s; John
Francis Rague, architect. Remodeled, rehabilitated, and west portico added
1921–24; Proudfoot, Bird and Rawson, architects. Under restoration 1972–76;
Prof. Margaret Keyes, The University of Iowa, consultant. Fine example of
the style. Served as third territorial capitol 1842–46 and as first state capitol
1846–57; first permanent building, The University of Iowa, 1857. 1 ext. photocopy (no date); HABSI forms (1957, 1967). NHL

Plum Grove (Gov. Robert Lucas House) (IA–41)
   1030 Carroll Ave.

Museum. Red brick, approximately 28' (three-bay front) x 44', two-story block with one-story rear ell, gable roof with gable end to street; side hall plan. Built ca. 1844 by Robert Lucas, first governor of Iowa Territory; altered in 1870s, including addition of west wing and raising roof of rear ell to one-and-a-half stories; restored 1943–46, including removal of wing and lowering of ell; F. L. Carnes, architect for State Conservation Commission; under further restoration since 1975, Wehner, Nowysz and Pattshull, architects. 1 ext. photo (1934, showing house before restoration); HABSI (1964). NR

Keosauqua   **Van Buren County (89)**

* *Pearson, Benjamin Franklin, House* (IA–122)   (Fig. 11)
   Dodge St. at NW corner of intersection with Country Rd.

Historic house museum of the Van Buren County Historical Society. Irregular limestone ashlar, light gray with brown ashlar trim at first story, red brick at second story, six-bay front, two stories, gable roof with sloping end parapets and paired end chimneys. Built 1845 by stone mason Benjamin Franklin Pearson; restored 1964; damaged by tornado and repaired 1967. Reputedly a stop on the Underground Railroad; top floor originally open and used for Methodist services. 2 ext. photos (1934).

Van Buren County Courthouse (IA–49)
   904 4th St.

Red brick, three bays (front) by four bays, two stories, gable roof with gable end forming pediment, wooden cornice with wide frieze, Greek Revival details; second floor courtroom. Built 1841–43 by Edwin Manning. 1 ext. photocopy (no date); HABSI (1964).

Knoxville Vicinity   **Marion County (63)**

* *Reichard, John, House* (IA–55)   (Fig. 66)
   About 3.5 mi. E of city and .7 mi. S of State Rte. 92 before relocation.

Red brick with limestone sills and basement, L-shaped plan, 36'-4" (three-bay front) x 36'-4", one-and-a-half stories, gable roofs with scrollwork eaves and bargeboards, entrance porch with scrollwork; central hall plan with kitchen wing at rear, Gothic Revival style. Built 1864 or 1865; interior remodeled 1964; demolished 1976 for highway construction. 7 sheets (1976†, including site plan, plans, section, details); 7 ext. photos (1976†), 1 int. photo (1976†); 23 data pages (1977†).

Le Claire   **Scott County (82)**

Cody, Isaac, House (IA–56)
   Originally at 1034 N. Cody St.; moved to Buffalo Bill Historical Center, 720 Sheridan Ave., Cody, Wyoming.

Museum. Wood frame with clapboards, rectangular plan with ell at rear (three-bay front), two stories with one-story ell, gable roof. Built ca. 1840; moved to Cody, Wyoming, early 1930s. Boyhood home of William F. ("Buffalo Bill") Cody. 1 photocopy (no date†).

Marietta   Marshall County (64)

Hicksite Friends Meetinghouse (IA–13)
   N side County Rd. E-29, about .5 mi. W of County Rd. 75. This intersection is 3 mi. S of Albion.

Wood frame and clapboard, six-bay front, one story, gable roof, porch at front and one side. Built 1860s or 1870s; burned ca. 1940. Graveyard extant. 1 ext. photo (1934).

Marshalltown   Marshall County (64)

* *First Church of Christ, Scientist* (IA–94)   (Fig. 97)
   SE corner W. Main and N. 5th St.

Stucco on wood frame, rubble-stone foundation, cross-shaped plan, approximately 52' x 64', one story, intersecting steep gable roofs, Prairie style. Built 1902–03; Hugh M. G. Garden, architect. 2 ext. photos (1977).

* *Marshall County Courthouse* (IA–78)   (Fig. 73)
   Square bounded by Center, Main, Church Sts., and First Ave.

Limestone with wood and sheet metal trim, lower floors rusticated, three stories on raised basement, hipped roof with prominent dormers and chimneys, sculpture group above central entrance pavilion, 175' central domed clock tower with lantern; domed interior rotunda, classical details. Built 1884–86, J. C. Cochrane of Chicago, architect. 1 ext. photo (1977). NR

Mason City   Cerro Gordo County (17)

* *City National Bank* (now Van Duyn's Clothing Store) (IA–79)   (Fig. 98)
   4 S. Federal Ave., SW corner Federal and W. State St.

Yellowish Roman brick with stone and terra cotta trim, five bays by nine bays, now three stories, low-pitched hipped roof with widely overhanging eaves, Prairie style. Built 1909–10; Frank Lloyd Wright, architect; originally two stories with a solid brick wall enclosing a tall banking room lighted by clerestory windows; converted to a store in 1930 by Des Moines architect E. F. Rasmussen, display windows added; banking room divided into two stories. Built as part of a commission which included the complementary Park Inn Hotel to the W. All original fixtures and furnishings were designed by Wright. A rare example of Wright's commercial architecture in the Prairie style. 1 ext. photo (1977); HABSI (1958). NR

* *Melson, Joshua G., House* (IA–95)   (Fig. 100)
   56 River Heights Dr.

Limestone rubble with concrete mullions and decorative keystones, approx-
imately 37′ x 61′, two stories with basement, hipped roof, grouped windows
and corner piers, open plan at first floor, Prairie style. Built in 1912–13; Walter
Burley Griffin, architect. Dramatically sited on limestone bluff in Rock Crest-
Rock Glen subdivision planned by Griffin to harmonize with landscape along
Willow Creek. Melson was one of four partners who developed Rock Crest-
Rock Glen. 2 ext. photos (1977), photocopy of presentation drawing (1912);
HABSI (1970).

Park Inn Hotel (IA–80)
   15 W. State St.

Yellowish Roman brick with stone and wood trim, rectangular first floor
covers entire lot, second and third floors are U-shaped, low-pitched hipped
roof with wide overhanging eaves, Prairie style. Built in 1909–10; Frank Lloyd
Wright, architect. Part of a single commission which included the adjacent
City National Bank. The only remaining hotel designed by Wright. 1 ext.
photo (1977); HABSI (1968). NR

* *Rule, Arthur L., House* (IA–57)   (Fig. 99)
   11 S. Rock Glen

Hollow clay tile with natural gray stucco, 42′-8″ x 60′-3″, two stories plus
basement, hipped roofs, horizontal trellises above first-floor windows,
grouped ornamental leaded-glass casements; open plan first floor, plan on 3′-
3″ module, Prairie style. Built 1913; Walter Burley Griffin, architect; second-
floor addition before 1934. In Rock Crest-Rock Glen subdivision planned by
Griffin. 1 ext. photo (1977†), 1 ext. photocopy (1913†); 20 data pages (1972†);
HABSI (1967).

Monroe   **Jasper County (50)**

Kling House (IA–33)
   416 N. Monroe St.

Brick with board-and-batten ell at rear, octagonal plan, two stories, mansard
roof, bracketed eaves and porch. Built late 19th c.; exterior stuccoed after 1934.
3 ext. photos (1934).

Mount Pleasant   **Henry County (44)**

**Iowa Insane Hospital* (now called State Mental Health Institute at Mount Pleas-
   ant), Main Building (IA–58)   (Fig. 44)
   U.S. Rte. 218, SE of town.

Coursed ashlar with rock-cut foundation, modified echelon plan about 760′
long consisting of two units on a central axis with symmetrical connected
wings in a step-back plan, two, three, and four stories, gable roofs with
cupolas, polygonal and round bay-window towers; central hall plan in each

unit. Built 1855–65; Jonathan Preston, architect; added to 1884–87; Willett and Pashley, architects for addition; demolished 1936 and later, except for part of rear-center building. First mental hospital in Iowa. 2 ext. photocopies (ca. 1930†), 2 int. photocopies (ca. 1895†), 2 photocopies of engraved views (ca. 1867†, ca. 1895†); 32 data pages (1974†).

* *Iowa Wesleyan College*(formerly Iowa Wesleyan University),*Old Main* (IA–59)
   S side Broad St. between Main and Broadway Sts.   (Fig. 47)

Yellow-brown brick with rubble foundation, 100' (nine-bay front) x 55', three stories, hipped roof, central domed cupola, first floor bays separated by brick pilasters; double-loaded corridor plan, Italianate style. Built 1854–55; Alexander Lee, contractor. 2 ext. photos (1974†, 1977†); 21 data pages (1974†). NR

* *Iowa Wesleyan College*(originally Mount Pleasant Collegiate Institute),*Pioneer Hall* (IA–60)   (Fig. 46)
   S side Broad St. between Main and Broadway Sts.

Red brick with rubble foundation, 54' (six-bay front) x 28', two stories, gable roof. Built 1843–45. First building on the Mount Pleasant campus and oldest collegiate building west of Mississippi. 2 ext. photos (1974†, 1977†), 1 ext. photocopy (19th c.†); 10 data pages (1974†).

Muscatine   **Muscatine County (70)**

Clark, Alexander, Houses (IA–107)
   307–09 Chestnut St.

Two frame houses joined by enclosed areaway, asphalt siding over original clapboards, each unit approx. 20' (three-bay front) x 25', two stories, gable roofs with ridges perpendicular; side hall plans. Built mid 19th c.; alterations and rear additions; porch added across front of both units; demolished 1975. Alexander Clark, nationally prominent Negro leader and U.S. minister to Liberia, owned these houses and lived in 309 in 1878–79 while rebuilding his adjacent home destroyed by fire. 6 ext. photocopies (1975†), 3 int. photocopies (1975†); 13 data pages (1975†).

Nashua Vicinity   **Chickasaw County (19)**

**Little Brown Church in the Vale* (originally First Congregational Church of Bradford, Iowa) (IA–20)   (Fig. 48)
   W side State Rte. 346, about 1 mi. E of Nashua.

Museum. Wood frame with brown-painted clapboards, 50'-4" x 26'-5" with 10'-1" x 10'-8" projecting entrance tower at gable end, one story, gable roof with hipped roof on tower. Built ca. 1860–64. Site inspired William S. Pitts's song, "The Church in the Wildwood." 9 sheets (1961, including plans, elevations, sections, details); 2 ext. photos (1977); 3 data pages (1961).

* *Nelson, Daniel, House* (IA–81)   (Fig. 12)
    S side of Glendale Rd., 1 mi. E of intersection with U.S. Rte. 63, about 3 mi.
    N of Oskaloosa.

Museum of the Mahaska County Historical Society. Red brick with stone
lintels and sills, L-shaped plan, five-bay front, two stories, gable roof, one-
story wooden porches on front and rear; central hall plan, built-in cupboards
and closets flanking fireplaces. Outbuildings to rear include summer kitchen
and privy, wood shed reconstructed 1964. Built 1853; restored 1964–65.
Remained in Nelson family until 1941. 6 ext. photos (1977, including outbuildings); HABSI (1964). NR

Nelson, Daniel, Barn (IA–81 A)
    N Side of Glendale Rd., 1 mi. E of intersection with U.S. Rte. 63, about 3
    mi. N of Oskaloosa.

Museum. Timber frame with board-and-batten siding, oak trees form corner
posts, 46' x 61', one story, gable roof, original lofts on west side only. Built
1856; some interior alterations for museum use. Originally used primarily for
grain storage. 2 ext. photos (1977). NR

Pella   **Marion Country (63)**

* *Central College, Temporary Quarters* (IA–96)   (Fig. 27)
    1107 W. Washington St.

Red brick, twelve-bay front, left five bays one story, right seven bays two stories in front and one story at rear, gable roofs, tumbled brick at gable ends, was
two buildings joined somewhat later by the two central bays, some plank-and-
beam floor construction. Built late 1840s. Tumbled brick and plank-and-beam
floor construction are Dutch construction practices. Temporary quarters for
Iowa Central University's (now Central College) first classes, 1854–56. 2 ext.
photos (1977).

* *Van Spankeren House* (Wyatt Earp House) (IA–97)   (Figs. 25, 26)
    507 E. Franklin St.

Museum, part of Pella Historical Village. Double house (two houses side by
side), white-painted brick, eight-bay front, two stories, gable roof, large windows; plank-and-beam floor construction. Built ca. 1850. Boyhood home of
Wyatt Earp. 1 ext. photo (1977); 2 int. photos (1977).

Roelofsz, Dr. Joost, House (Viersen House) (IA–32)
    1008–10 Main St. (originally Reformation Ave.)

Stuccoed brick, central block with side kitchen and office wings, one-and-a-
half stories, steep gambrel roofs, wooden trellis porches, applied Gothic details. Built 1848 by Dr. Roelofsz, one of original Dutch immigrants to Pella and
town's first doctor. House contained his office and painting studio. Remained

in daughter's (Viersen) family until demolition in 1934. Replica built 1975–76 by Paul Vande Noord for Pella Historical Village, Franklin Ave. between E. First and E. Second Sts. 2 ext. photos (1934); 2 data pages (1977).

Red Oak   Montgomery County (69)

* *Montgomery County Courthouse* (IA–98)   (Fig. 74)
 Courthouse Square

Rock-faced white limestone first floor and basement, red pressed brick above, rectangular plan, three-and-a-half stories plus basement, hipped roof with gables at projecting bays, six-story corner tower with clock, Richardson Romanesque style. Cornerstone laid 1890. 2 ext. photos (1977).

Rock Rapids   Lyon County (60)

Reinforced Concrete Arch Bridge (Melan Bridge) (IA–61)
 Originally spanning Dry Creek, now in Emma Sater Park on N side of State Rte. 9 at E edge of town.

Reinforced concrete elliptical arch, jasper spandrels, 30' span, 6'-6" rise of arch. Built 1893 for state highway in vicinity; moved 1964; no longer in use. Designed by German-born engineer Fritz von Emperger; used system of reinforcing invented by Austrian engineer Joseph Melan. One of earliest bridges of its type in the United States. 2 photocopies (1959†); 8 data pages (no date†). NR

Saint Donatus   Jackson Country (49)

* *Frank Stephen, House* (IA–17)   (Figs. 29, 30, 31)
 .3 mi. W of crossroads at center of town, on road parallel and just N of County Rd. D–53.

Stuccoed stone, 40' (five-bay front) x 25' with 14'-3" x 25' barn attached at side, house two stories, barn one story, jerkin-head house roof, lean-to barn roof, side lights and transom at front entrance with carved door panels; central hall plan. Built mid 19th c.; attributed to John Beckius; front entrance removed after 1934, makeshift replacement; barn replaced by garage. 2 sheets (1934, including plans, elevations, details); 1 ext. photo (1934), 1 int. photo (1934).

Sheldahl   Story County (85)

* *First Evangelical Lutheran Church* (now called Sheldahl Norwegian Lutheran Church) (IA–62)   (Fig. 68)
 Two blocks E of County Rd. R-38 and one block N of NW. 166 Ave.

Wood frame with clapboards, 28'-5" (one-bay front) x 30'-8", one story, gable roof, simple belfry, original furnishings. Built 1883 by Osmund Sheldahl. 4 sheets (1956†, including site map, plan, elevations, details); 1 ext. photo (1974†), 3 int. photos (1974†); 10 data pages (1974†); HABSI (1971).

Sioux City   **Woodbury County (97)**

* *Woodbury County Courthouse* (IA–82)   (Figs. 101, 102, 103)
  Seventh and Douglas Sts.

Tan Roman brick with matching terra cotta trim, gray granite base and copings, large two-story rectangular block with central office tower rising six more stories, rhythmic windows separated by vertical piers, sculptural figures at monumental main entrances; interior rotunda with stained-glass dome, lavish use of Sullivanesque terra cotta ornament, large murals. Built 1916–18; Purcell and Elmslie and William Steele, architects; George G. Elmslie, principal designer; Alfonso Iannelli, sculptor; John W. Norton, muralist. An important monument of early modern architecture and one of the largest Prairie style buildings ever erected. 14 ext. photos (1976), 8 int. photos (1976); HABSI forms (1964, 1968). NR

Spirit Lake, Dickinson County. See Arnolds Park, Dickinson County

Springdale   **Cedar County (16)**

* *Maxson, William, House* (John Brown House) (IA–16)   (Figs. 33, 34, 35)
  1.5 mi. N of Springdale exit from Interstate 80 on County Rd. X-40, then 1.5 mi. E on unmarked county road, then .2 mi. N on unmarked county road.

Stuccoed stone, 34'-5" (three-bay front) x 26'-10", one-and-a-half stories, gable roof, two entrance doors with side lights; rooms form U centered around rear porch, Greek Revival style. Built mid 19th c.; evidence of two ells at rear; demolished 1934. John Brown's men stayed here while training for attack on Harpers Ferry, Oct. 16, 1859. 8 sheets (1934, including plans, elevations, section, details); 8 ext. photos (1934, showing house in ruinous condition).

Valley Junction   **Polk County (77)**

Clegg House. See West Des Moines. The name of the town was changed in 1938 from Valley Junction to West Des Moines.

Vandalia   **Jasper County (50)**

* *Pulver House* (IA–1)   (Figs. 21, 22, 23)
  On N side of road leading E from town. Vandalia is in SE Jasper County, 1.3 mi. N of County Rd. F-70 and 2.7 mi. E of State Rte. 316.

Frame with clapboards above rubble-stone basement, 28'-2" (front) x 44'-2", one-and-a-half stories above raised basement, gable roof; irregular room placement within regular plan. Built about 1848; attributed to Daniel Ferdinand Pulver; demolished. 9 sheets (1934, including plans, elevations, details); 5 ext. photos (1934).

Vinton   **Benton County (6)**

*Iowa Institution for the Education of the Blind (now Iowa Braille and Sight Saving
  School) (IA–63)   (Fig. 45)
  1002 G Ave.

Light-colored limestone ashlar above rock-faced basement, 273' (22-bay front) x 112', three stories, hipped and gable roofs, central cupola, wooden verandas at wings, shaped sheet-metal cornices; cast iron interior stairways, Italianate style. Central portion built 1858–62; south wing built 1868–69; north wing built 1872–73. Robert S. Finkbine and Chauncey F. Lovelace, architects for central portion and south wing; George Josselyn prepared plans for north wing. Interior remodeling, auditorium, and new front porch 1913 or after; Proudfoot, Bird and Rawson, architects. Appears to be oldest state institution building surviving in Iowa next to "Old Capitol." 1 ext. photocopy (20th c.†), photocopy of engraving (1875†), 6 photocopies of measured drawings (elevation and plans, 1913†), 23 data pages (1974†).

Waterloo   **Black Hawk County (7)**

House (IA–101)

Frame, narrow dark-stained siding on first floor, shingles on second, rectangular two-and-a-half story block with one-story wings and porch, hipped roof with low dormers, broad overhanging eaves, grouped windows with leaded panes on first floor, Prairie style. Built ca. 1911; Mortimer B. Cleveland, architect. 1 ext. photocopy (1912†), photocopy of floor plan (1912†).

* *Russell, Rensselaer, House* (IA–64)   (Fig. 36)
   520 W. 3rd St.

Historic house museum. Red brick, irregular plan about 53' (five-bay front) x 50', two stories plus cellar, hipped roofs, cupola; central hall plan, Italianate style. Built 1862–63; remodeled 1947; restored 1969–72. 2 ext. photos (1973†, 1977†); 2 int. photos (1973†); 15 data pages (1974†). HABSI (1972). NR

Webster City   **Hamilton County (40)**
* *Kendall Young Library* (IA–102)   (Fig. M-17)
   1201 Wilson St.

Brick with limestone trim, rectangular plan, one story on raised basement, hipped tile roof, central entrance flanked by paired Ionic columns supporting elaborate pediment, rusticated quoining, balustrade at eaves, Beaux Arts style. Built 1904; Patton and Miller, architects. 1 ext. photocopy (1904†).

West Amana   **Iowa County (48)**

West Amana Flour Mill (IA–45)

Wood frame with clapboards, L-shaped plan, two-and-a-half stories with one-and-a-half story ell, gable roofs with dormers, tall masonry chimney at a distance to rear. Built ca. 1860; demolished after 1934. 1 ext. photo (1934).

West Branch   **Cedar County (16)**

* *Friends Meetinghouse* (IA–25)   (Figs. 49, 50)
   E side Downey St., S of Wapsinonoc Creek, Herbert Hoover National Historic Site. Original location on Downey St., two blocks N of present site.

Museum of the National Park Service. Wood frame with clapboards, 50'-2" (six-bay front) x 30'-1", one story, gable roof with shed-roofed side addition, two symmetrical doors; open plan with central partition of sliding panels separating men's and women's sections. Built 1855–57; remodeled 1880s; moved across street and converted to theater in 1915; moved and extensively restored 1964–65; William J. Wagner, architect; sliding partition and benches came from contemporary Hickory Grove Meetinghouse at Scattergood School; side porch and cry room-privy came from 1880s Conservative Friends Meetinghouse in West Branch. Attended by Herbert Hoover as a boy. 11 sheets (1964†, including site plan, plans, elevations, details); 6 ext. photocopies (ca. 1963† before restoration, ca. 1965†, 1977†), 1 int. photocopy (1977†).

* *Hoover, Herbert, Birthplace* (Jesse Hoover House) (IA–21)   (Figs. 8, 9)
   SW corner Penn and Downey Sts., Herbert Hoover National Historic Site.

House Museum of the National Park Service. Board-and-batten cabin, 20'-4" (three-bay front) x 20'-10" including partly-enclosed rear porch, gable roof; two rooms, vertical board interior walls. Built ca. 1871; moved and attached to rear of two-story house in 1885; returned to original location and restored in 1938 by McKay Construction Co.; further restoration 1962, William J. Wagner, architect. Birthplace of 31st president of the United States. 4 sheets (1964, including site plan, plans, elevations, sections, details); 8 ext. photocopies (ca. 1962†), 1 int. photocopy (1977†); HABSI (no date).

West Des Moines   Polk County (77)

* *Clegg House* (IA–7)   (Fig. 65)
   Corner of 6th St. and Ashworth Rd.

Concrete on stone foundation, octagonal, 39'-6" across, two stories, nearly flat hipped roof. Probably built 1865; demolished after 1934. 9 sheets (1934, including plans, elevations, section, details); 2 ext. photos (1934).

Winterset   Madison County (61)

Clark, Caleb, House (IA–65)
   814 S. 8th Ave., about a block S of Summit St.

Limestone, irregular ashlar and rubble, L-shaped plan, one story, gable roofs. Built 1854–55; demolished after 1960. 2 ext. photos (1959, 1964), 3 photocopies of measured drawings (1960†); 4 data pages (1960†); HABSI (1957).

* *Madison County Courthouse* (IA–83)   (Fig. 72)
   Courthouse Square.

Light beige limestone ashlar, Greek cross plan, 100' x 100' (five bays on all sides), identical facades with pediments and one-story entrance piazzas, two stories, cross-gable roof, tall octagonal dome with iron framing and sheet metal covering; brick shallow-arched floor construction carried on cast-iron beams, Renaissance Revival details. Built 1876–77 on foundations of earlier courthouse destroyed by fire; A.H. Piquenard, architect; courthouse remodeled ca. 1960s. 1 ext. photo (1977†), 1 ext. photocopy (no date†), 1 int. photocopy of tower construction (1971†); 15 data pages (1972†). NR

Appendix

Buildings Recorded on
HISTORIC AMERICAN BUILDINGS SURVEY
Inventory Forms

The following buildings were recorded on the one-page Historic American Building Survey Inventory forms. The inventory program was initiated in 1953 by the American Institute of Architects, the National Trust for Historic Preservation, and the National Park Service to fill the hiatus created by lack of post-war funding for HABS. When HABS was reactivated, the inventory became an adjunct to its comprehensive recording program. Need for the inventory program declined with the growth of state-sponsored surveys under the National Historic Preservation Act of 1966, and it was discontinued in 1970. The brief forms were designed to be filled out by laymen, and most of those now on file are the result of voluntary efforts by interested individuals and preservation groups. The names, addresses, architects, and dates given below are those which appear on the inventory forms and have not been verified by the catalog compiler. Those buildings marked with a † are more fully documented in the HABS archives and can be found listed in the main body of the catalog. HABSI forms are filed in the Prints and Photographs Division of the Library of Congress from which reproductions can be ordered.

ADEL   *Dallas County (25)*

Adel Presbyterian Church (now Public Library), 820 Prairie St. (1868). HABSI form (1960).

Dallas County Courthouse, City Square, Main St. between 7th and 8th Sts. (1902, Proudfoot & Bird). HABSI form (1958).

ALBIA   *Monroe County (68)*

Monroe County Courthouse, Square bounded by S. Main St., S. Clinton St., Washington Ave. E., and Benton Ave. E. (1903, O. O. Smith). HABSI form (1968).

ALLISON   *Butler County (12)*

Butler County Courthouse, N. Main and 6th Sts. (1881). HABSI form (1971).

Haines, Thomas E., House, 202 2nd St., SE. (1878). HABSI form (1970).

AMES *Story County (85)*

Ames City Armory (O'Neil Dairy Building), 308 5th St. (1905). HABSI form (1971).

Budd, J. L., House, 804 Kellogg Ave. (1885). HABSI form (1970).

Chicago and Northwestern Passenger Station, W. Main and Clark Sts. (1900, Frost & Granger). 4 HABSI forms (1968).

Dunagan, Walter, House, 3424 Oakland St. (1940, Souer & Emery). HABSI form (1968).

Greeley, Capt. W. M., House (Adams Mortuary), 502 Douglas St. (late 19th c.). HABSI form (1968).

Hubbell, Lois W., House, 525 Welch Ave. (1914). HABSI form (1970).

Iowa State University, Alumni Hall, Union Dr. (1904, Proudfoot & Bird). HABSI form (1967).

Iowa State University, Engineering Annex, Riggs Ct. and Marston Ct. (1910, Proudfoot, Bird & Rawson). HABSI form (1968).

Iowa State University, English Office Building, Morrill Rd. (1884, Foster and Liebbe). HABSI form (1967).

†Iowa State University, Farm House, 40' W of Knoll Rd., adjoining central campus. (1860–65, Milens Burt). HABSI form (1967).

Iowa State University, Hall of Agriculture (Curtiss Hall), Knoll Rd. (1909, Proudfoot & Bird). HABSI form (1968).

Iowa State University, Landscape Architecture Building, Knoll Road. (1900, Liebbe, Nourse & Rasmussen). HABSI form (1967).

Iowa State University, Old Botany Hall, NE edge of central campus. (1892, Josselyn & Taylor). HABSI form (1967).

Munn, H. L., and Son, 102 E. Main St. (1891). HABSI form (1970).

Pope, Alexander, House (Iowa State University, Music Department Annex), 2154 Lincoln Way. (1877). HABSI form (1967).

Sigma Alpha Epsilon Fraternity House, 140 Lynn Ave. (1928–29, Kimball, Cowgill & Baity). HABSI form (1968).

Sigma Chi Fraternity House, 125 N. Hyland Ave. (ca. 1920). HABSI form (1972).

Starr, Dr. Samuel J., House (the Octagon Art Gallery), 126 Sumner St. (1870). HABSI form (1967).

Taylor, Harvey N., House, 1006 Lincoln Way. (1860s). HABSI form (1967).

AMES VICINITY *Boone County (8)*

Luther, Clark, House, Rte. 17, 6 mi. S of intersection with U.S. Rte. 30, 12 mi. SW of Ames. (1853–56). HABSI form (1972).

ANAMOSA   *Jones County (53)*

Iowa State Men's Reformatory, off U.S. Rte. 64 and 151, N of Courthouse. (1880–92). HABSI form (no date).

BELLEVUE   *Jackson County (49)*

Mont Rest (Seth L. Baker House), NW corner 3rd and Spring Sts. (1893). HABSI form (1972).

BLOOMFIELD   *Davis County (25)*

Davis County Courthouse, Courthouse Square. (1877, T. J. Tolan and Sons). HABSI form (1968).

BLUE GRASS   *Scott County (82)*

Blackman-Carstens House. (prior to 1840). HABSI form (1957).

BENTONSPORT   *Van Buren County (89)*

†Hancock House, SW corner 3rd and Walnut Sts. (1850s, James Brown). HABSI form (1964).

Mason, J. L., House. (1840s). HABSI form (1957).

†Post Office, Front St. (ca. 1840s). HABSI form (1964).

BOONE   *Boone County (8)*

†City Hall, SE corner 8th and Allen Sts. (1874–75). HABSI form (1971).

Commercial Buildings (Hamilton Hardware Store and Junior Miss Fashions), 710–14 Story St. (1884–86). HABSI form (1970).

Eckstein House, 1815 Story St. (1894, 1900). HABSI form (1971).

First National Bank, 8th and Story Sts. (1916, Woodburn & Son). HABSI form (1968).

Herman, John H., House, 711 S. Story St. (1919, Proudfoot, Bird & Rawson). HABSI form (1970).

Olson, Leonard, House, 421 S. Marshall St. (1932, Vorse, Kraetsch & Kraetsch). HABSI form (1972).

Sacred Heart Church, 12th and Marshall Sts. (1891). HABSI form (1967).

Shelders, Jacob M., House, 303 Crawford. (1871). HABSI form (1967).

Sparks, Clyde, House, 408 S. Story St. (1917, E. V. Fitzgerald). HABSI form (1968).

CARROLL   *Carroll County (14)*

Carroll Public Library, NW corner 6th and Court Sts. (1905, Thomas R. Kimball). HABSI form (no date).

CEDAR FALLS   *Blackhawk County (7)*

Jamerson, Robert, House, 1020 Franklin St. (1915). HABSI form (1969).

"Old Pickle Factory," on S bank of Cedar River W of Main St. Bridge. (ca. 1860). HABSI form (1970).

CEDAR FALLS VICINITY   *Blackhawk County (7)*

Fields Barn (Uhl Barn), Rte. 57, 1.25 mi. SW of intersection with Rte. 58. (1875). HABSI form (1960).

CEDAR RAPIDS   *Linn County (57)*

Calder Houses, 1214–16 Second Ave. SE. (1860s). HABSI form (1968).

Peoples Savings Bank, 3rd Ave. and 1st St., SW. (1911, Louis Sullivan). HABSI form (1968).

St. Paul's Methodist Church, NW corner 3rd Ave. and 14th St., SE. (1913–14, Louis Sullivan and Purcell and Elmslie). 2 HABSI forms (1968, no date).

CERES   *Clayton County (22)*

St. Peter's German United Evangelical Church (Pioneer Rock Church), U.S. Rte. 52. (1858). HABSI form (no date).

CHARLES CITY   *Floyd County (34)*

First Methodist Church, NE corner Kelly and Wisconsin Sts. (1867–69). HABSI form (1966).

First National Bank, 223 N. Main St. (1871–72). HABSI form (1966).

Gilbert, Milo, House, 307 N. Jackson St. (ca. 1863). HABSI form (1966).

Gilbert's Stone Block, 119–23 N. Main St. (1863, 1877). HABSI form (1966).

Smith, Dr. Joel W., House (Elks Club), 418 Wisconsin St. (1874). HABSI form (1966).

CLERMONT VICINITY   *Fayette County (33)*

†Montauk (Gov. William Larrabee House), U.S. Rte. 18, one mi. NE of Clermont. (1874, Edward Townsend Mix). HABSI form (1970).

CLINTON   *Clinton County (23)*

†Clinton County Courthouse, Courthouse Square. (1892–97, G. Stanley Mansfield). HABSI form (1968).

Curtis, George M., House (Clinton Women's Club), 420 5th Ave., S. (1880). HABSI form (1962).

†Van Allen, John D., Store (Petersen, Harned and Von Maur), 200 5th Ave., S. (1913–15, Louis Sullivan). HABSI form (1962).

CORNING VICINITY   *Adams County (2)*

Frank, George W., House (Edgewood Estate, now Happy Hollow Country Club), 1 mi. E of Corning, off old U.S. Rte. 34. (early 1880s). HABSI form (1967).

CRESTON   *Union County (88)*

C. B. & Q. Railroad Depot, Adams and Maple Sts. (1898–99). HABSI form (1968).

CROTON *Lee County (56)*

Crow, Lewis, House (Sprouse House), SE corner First and Walnut Sts. (ca. 1845). HABSI form (1959).

DAVENPORT *Scott County (82)*

French, Judge Nathaniel, House, 20 Forest Rd. (1912–14, Temple, Burrows & McLane). HABSI form (1970).

J. H. C. Petersen's Sons Company (Petersen, Harned and Von Maur), 219 W. 2nd St. (1892, F. G. Clausen). HABSI form (1972).

DECORAH *Winneshiek County (77)*

Arlington House (Norwegian-American Museum), 520 W. Water St. (1876). HABSI form (1971).

DES MOINES *Polk County (77)*

Capital City State Bank, E. Locust and E. 5th Sts. (1903). HABSI form (1968).

Central Christian Church, 9th and Pleasant Sts. (1889–90, Foster & Liebbe). 2 HABSI forms (1962, 1970).

Chamberlain Hotel, NE corner 7th and Locust Sts. (1903). HABSI form (1967).

Clifton Heights Presbyterian Church, 1931 SW. First St. (1923–24, F. A. Harris). HABSI form (1970).

Davidson Building, NW corner 8th and Walnut Sts. (1908–11). HABSI form (1968).

Finkbine, Robert S., House, 1915 Grand Ave. (ca. 1890, Robert S. Finkbine). HABSI form (1970).

McCune, C. A., House, 1719 Arlington St. (1906). HABSI form (1967).

Naylor, Thomas, House, 944 W. 9th St. (1869). HABSI form (1964).

Redhead, Wesley, House, 1757 Dean Ave. (1867, William Foster). HABSI form (no date).

Redhead, Wesley, Barn, 1757 Dean Ave. (1867, William Foster). HABSI form (1957).

Rose Hill (Hill Top), 3111 Easton Blvd. (1846). HABSI form (1958).

St. Mary's Roman Catholic Church, 2nd Ave. and Crocker St. (1874–76). HABSI form (1962).

St. Paul's Episcopal Church, 8th and High Sts. (1885, Foster & Liebbe). HABSI form (1957).

Scoville, Tyler, House (Ebersole's Aquarium), 620 E. 6th St. (1880). HABSI form (1962).

†Terrace Hill (Allen-Hubbell House), 2300 Grand Ave. (1867–69, W. W. Boyington). 2 HABSI forms (no date, 1967).

DEXTER VICINITY *Adair County (1)*

Mount Vernon Methodist Church, 4 mi. S and 2 mi. E of Dexter. (1890). HABSI form (1957).

119

DUBUQUE   *Dubuque County (31)*

†City Hall, 50 W. 13th St. (1857–58, John Francis Rague). HABSI form (1969).

†Dubuque County Courthouse, 720 Central Ave. (1891–93, Fridolin Heer & Son). HABSI form (no date).

†Dubuque County Jail, 36 E. 8th St. (1857–58, John Francis Rague). HABSI form (1969).

Goodrich-Wilson-Ryan House, 1243 Locust St. (ca. 1857, attributed to John Francis Rague). HABSI form (1969).

St. Raphael's Cathedral, 1300 Main St. (1857–61). HABSI form (1970).

†Shot Tower, Commercial St. near E end of E. 4th St. (1856, C. H. Rogers & Co.). HABSI form (no date).

Third Ward School (Prescott Apartments), 1195 Central Ave. (1857, John Francis Rague). HABSI form (1969).

ELDON   *Wapello County (90)*

Dibble House (American Gothic House, P. Wilbor Smith House), NW corner Gothic (Hearn) and Burton Sts. (ca. 1860s). HABSI form (1962).

EMMETSBURG   *Palo Alto County (74)*

Sanders, William E., House, Oakwood Dr. (1896). HABSI form (1970).

ESTHERVILLE   *Emmet County (32)*

Brown, A. C., House, 1421 First Ave., S. (1904). HABSI form (1967).

FLORIS VICINITY   *Davis County (26)*

†Mars Hill Baptist Church, approx. 4 mi. NE of Floris. (ca. 1850). HABSI form (1956).

FOREST CITY   *Winnebago County (95)*

Winnebago County Courthouse, Clark St. between I and J Sts. (1896, Kinney & Orth). HABSI form (1970).

FORT DODGE   *Webster County (94)*

Corey, Frank, House, 1238 6th Ave., N. (1913). HABSI form (1970).

FORT MADISON   *Lee County (56)*

Atlee-Waldan House, 802 Ave., E. (1860s) HABSI form (1970).

GLENWOOD   *Mills County (65)*

Mills County Courthouse, Courthouse Square. (1857). HABSI form (1957).

GREENE   *Butler County (12)*

Coldwater Church of the Brethren, High St., W of intersection with Old Rte. 14. (1873, William Bauchman). HABSI form (1968).

GREENFIELD   *Adair County (1)*

Warren Opera House, Public Square. (1896, Bell and Kent). HABSI form (1970).

GRINNELL   *Poweshiek County (79)*

†Merchants' National Bank (Poweshiek County National Bank), NW corner Fourth Ave. and Broad St. (1914, Louis Sullivan). HABSI form (1967).

GRUNDY CENTER   *Grundy County (38)*

Grundy County Courthouse, Courthouse Square between G and H Aves. and 7th and 8th Sts. (1891, Kramer & Zoll). HABSI form (1967).

Quick, Herbert, School, G Ave. in City Park. (ca. 1860–65). HABSI form (1958).

GRUNDY CENTER VICINITY   *Grundy County (38)*

Ayers, Samuel, House (Herbert Quick House), approx. 7 mi. NE of Grundy Center. (1867). HABSI form (1959).

HAMPTON   *Franklin County (35)*

Franklin County Courthouse (Third), Courthouse Square, Central Ave. and First St., NW. (1890–99, T. D. Allen). HABSI form (1970).

Hampton Memorial Hall, NE corner 5th and Main Sts. (1890). HABSI form (1970).

HAMPTON VICINITY   *Franklin County (35)*

Maysville Schoolhouse, only structure remaining from Maysville, .25 mi. off U.S. Rte. 65, 6 mi. S of Hampton. (1866). HABSI form (1970).

INDEPENDENCE   *Buchanan County (10)*

Rush Park Show Barn, NW corner intersection U.S. Rte. 20 and State Rte. 248. (1890, S. C. Sunderland). HABSI form (1967).

IOWA CITY   *Johnson County (52)*

First Presbyterian Church, 26 E. Market St. (1844). HABSI form (1957).

†Old Capitol (Third Territorial and First State Capitol), Dubuque St. and Iowa Ave. (1840–50s, John Francis Rague). 2 HABSI forms (1957, 1967).

†Plum Grove (Gov. Robert Lucas House), 1030 Carroll Ave. (ca. 1844). HABSI form (1964).

Wood, Grant, House, 1142 E. Court St. (1858). HABSI form (1959).

JOHNSTON   *Polk County (77)*

Trier, Dr. Paul J., House, 6880 NW. Bever Dr. (1958, Frank Lloyd Wright). HABSI form (1968).

KEOKUK   *Lee County (56)*

Keokuk Fire Station, 17 N. 6th St. (1856). HABSI form (1957).

121

Lee County Courthouse (South), 5th and Concert Sts. (1857, W. A. Rice). HABSI form (1958).

Union Agricultural and Stock Association, Old Plank Rd. (1869). HABSI form (1957).

KEOSAUQUA   Van Buren County (89)

†Van Buren County Courthouse, 904 4th St., overlooking Des Moines River. (1841–43, Edwin Manning). HABSI form (1964).

Hotel Manning, River St. (1854, 1893). HABSI form (1957).

KEOTA VICINITY   Keokuk County (54)

Maple Villa (S. Omar Singmaster House), off Rte. 77, 2 mi. N of Keota. (1917–18). HABSI form (1970).

LAMONI   Decatur County (27)

Liberty Hall, .75 mi. W of Rte. 69. (1881, Thomas Jacobs). HABSI form (1960).

LE MARS   Plymouth County (75)

Flaugher, Charles, House, SE corner First Ave. SW. and 6th St. (1890, Zack Eyres). HABSI form (1970).

MARSHALLTOWN   Marshall County (64)

First Baptist Church, 12 N. Second St. (1910, Harry W. Jones). HABSI form (1968).

Public Library, 10 N. Center St. (1902, Patton & Miller). HABSI form (1968).

MASON CITY   Cerro Gordo County (17)

†City National Bank (now Van Duyn's Clothing Store), 4 S. Federal Ave. (1909–10, Frank Lloyd Wright). HABSI form (1958).

Franke-Evans House, 507 E. State St. in Rock Crest-Rock Glen Subdivision. (1917, Francis Barry Byrne). HABSI form (1967).

†Melson House, 56 River Heights Dr. (1912–13, Walter Burley Griffin). HABSI form (1970).

†Park Inn Hotel, 15 W. State St. (1909–10, Frank Lloyd Wright). HABSI form (1968).

†Rule, Arthur, House, 11 S. Rock Glen. (1912, Walter Burley Griffin). HABSI form (1967).

MASSILLON   Cedar County (16)

Diamond Community Church, originally located in Jones Co., moved to Massillon in 1894. (1869). HABSI form (1970).

MITCHELLVILLE   Polk County (77)

Universalist Church, 4th and Market Sts. (1870). HABSI form (1964).

MONTROSE   Lee County (56)

St. Barnabas Episcopal Church, River Rd. between 3rd and 4th Sts. (1867–72). HABSI form (1962).

MOUNT PLEASANT   *Henry County (44)*

Harlan, James, House (Harlan-Lincoln House), 101 W. Broad St., N end of Main St. (mid 19th c.). HABSI form (1962).

MUSCATINE   *Muscatine County (70)*

Bishop, Will, House, 414 W. Second St. (1883, George P. Stauduhar). HABSI form (1968).

NEVADA   *Story County (85)*

Child, Capt. George, House (Wayne Wiley House), 807 Second St. (1854). HABSI form (1967).

Story County Courthouse, Main St. (1876, William Foster). HABSI form (1967).

NICHOLS   *Muscatine County (70)*

Nichols, Townsend, House, High and Nichols Sts. (1897, Henry Zeidler). HABSI form (1970).

OSKALOOSA VICINITY   *Mahaska County (62)*

†Nelson, Daniel, Farm, Glendale Rd. 3 mi. N of Oskaloosa. (1853). HABSI form (1964).

OTTUMWA   *Wapello County (90)*

Johnston, Allen, House, 531 N. Court St. (ca. 1882, Edward Clark). HABSI form (1967).

PELLA VICINITY   *Mahaska County (62)*

Smith, John, House, 5 mi. SE of Pella. (1869). HABSI form (1967).

Vorhees, John, House, 4.5 mi. SE of Pella. (1871). HABSI form (1962).

POLK CITY   *Polk County (77)*

Armstrong, Dr. Robert B., Office, Main St. (ca. 1875). HABSI form (1970).

POSTVILLE   *Allamakee County (3)*

St. Paul's Evangelical Lutheran Church, 401 S. Lawler. (1890–91). HABSI form (1971).

ROWAN   *Wright County (99)*

Rowen, Robert, House, SW of Rowan. (1857). HABSI form (1958).

SALEM   *Henry County (44)*

Lewelling, Henderson, House, SW side of Salem. (1840–45). HABSI form (1971).

SELMA VICINITY   *Van Buren County (89)*

Saylor, Thomas Benjamin, House (Hinkle Cabin), .5 mi. SE of Selma. (1835). HABSI form (1960).

SHELDAHL   *Story County (85)*

†First Evangelical Lutheran Church, two blocks E of county Rd. R-38 and one block N of NW. 166 Ave. (1883, Osmund Sheldahl). HABSI form (1971).

SIOUX CITY   *Woodbury County (97)*
†Woodbury County Courthouse, Seventh and Douglas Sts. (1916–18, William Steele and Purcell & Elmslie). 2 HABSI forms (1964, 1968).

SPIRIT LAKE   *Dickinson County (30)*

Dickinson County Courthouse, SE corner U.S. Rte. 9 and Hill St. (1890, Truman D. Allen). HABSI form (1968).

Johnson, A. M., building, 1724 Hill St. (1894). HABSI form (1971).

STUART VICINITY   *Guthrie County (39)*

Hollingsworth House, U.S. Rte. 90, W of Stuart. (1883). HABSI form (1964).

WATERLOO   *Blackhawk County (7)*

†Russell, Rensselaer, House, 520 W. 3rd St. (1862–63). HABSI form (1972).

St. Joseph's Church, 320 Mulberry. (1900, Murphy & Ralston). HABSI form (1970).

WAUBEEK VICINITY   *Linn County (57)*

Taylor Log House, Howard Cherry Boy Scout Reservation. (ca. 1880). HABSI form (1970).

WEBSTER CITY   *Hamilton County (40)*

Hamilton County Courthouse, Des Moines and Bank Sts. (1874–77, Street & Baker). HABSI form (1970).

WEST BEND   *Palo Alto County (74)*

Grotto of the Redemption, Broadway St., N of SS. Peter and Paul Church. (1912–1950s). HABSI form (1964).

WEST BRANCH   *Cedar County (16)*

†Hoover, Herbert, Birthplace, SW corner Penn and Downey Sts. (ca. 1871). HABSI form (no date).

Hoover, Jesse, Blacksmith Shop, SW corner Penn and Downey Sts. (reconstructed 1957, William J. Wagner). HABSI form (1957).

WEST CHESTER VICINITY   *Washington County (92)*

Kleese, Isaac, Farm, on County Rd., 3.25 mi. SE of West Chester. (mid 19th c.). HABSI form (1964).

WHAT CHEER   *Keokuk County (54)*

Masonic Opera House (What Cheer Opera House), 201 Barnes St. (1893). HABSI form (1968).

WINTERSET   *Madison County (61)*
†Clark, Caleb, House, 814 S. 8th Ave. (1854–55). HABSI form (1957).

124

A SURVEY OF STYLES

Todd R. Mozingo

A fuller treatment of architectural styles can be found in *What Style Is It?* by John Poppeliers, S. Allen Chambers, and Nancy B. Schwartz (Washington, D.C.: Preservation Press of the National Trust for Historic Preservation).

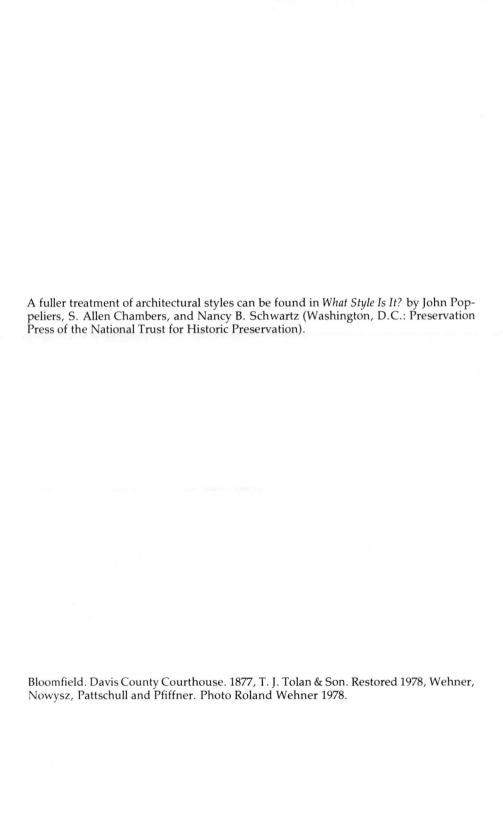

Bloomfield. Davis County Courthouse. 1877, T. J. Tolan & Son. Restored 1978, Wehner, Nowysz, Pattschull and Pfiffner. Photo Roland Wehner 1978.

A Survey of Styles

STYLISTIC categories are convenient labels given to buildings which share certain common characteristics. In various periods different historical styles have become popular according to the fashion and mood of the time. Thus it is important to understand what an architectural style is and how it reflects on the creation of architecture. Unlike flower identification, where one is concerned with identification of discrete species, buildings and their architectural styles are aesthetic creations. Not only may buildings vary in as many ways as they appear to be similar and still be considered to be of the same style, but an architectural style possesses a limitless capacity for hybridization.

To understand architectural styles, it is necessary to understand two pairs of terms and their interrelationship. The first is the concept of high style and vernacular, and the second is pure style and eclectic; in each case the pairs constitute opposites. High style is the ultimate in architectural sophistication, where the greatest attention is given to detail and a conscious effort is made to place the aesthetic goals of the design ahead of all other determinants. The vernacular tradition is the non-self-conscious tradition of architectural design where simple practicality is the central goal. The second pair of terms has a similar polar quality of meaning. Pure style is the use of the stylistic details and elements which are from only one tradition, exclusive of all others. The use of design elements from various stylistic traditions in a singular building is eclecticism. These four terms in their two functional pairs of opposites provide a framework for studying the hybridization of architectural styles. Every building's architectural style is to a large degree determined by the location that building holds in the continuums of high style to vernacular and pure style to eclectic.

This stylistic guide to architecture will not make an expert of a reader, nor is it an end in itself, for the study of architectural style is only meaningful if it is used as a component in the over-all study of architecture.

This style guide deals only with Iowa. For that reason, one will find no mention of eighteenth- or early nineteeth-century architecture. The cutoff period chosen is the beginning of "modern architecture" in the state—a date roughly corresponding with the beginning of the Second World War. What this guide does cover is a one hundred year period beginning with the initial settlement of Iowa—a century which may quite possibly encompass the greatest variety and richness of architectural expression in modern times, and in Iowa evidence of this full range is to be found.

References to Figure illustrations in this section are to the "Historic Architecture in Iowa" section, unless the Figure number is preceded by an M (for Mozingo). These latter illustrations are found in this section.

GREEK REVIVAL

Greek revival, the earliest architectural style which exists with any regularity in Iowa, was popular in the state from the period of early settlement until the Civil War. On a philosophical level, the Greek revival style in America was

Fig. M-1. Fort Madison. Lee County Courthouse. Photo Robert Thall 1976.

largely an attempt to link our new republic with the world's oldest, but it was also part of an international interest in the ancient Greeks stirred by archaeological discoveries.

The ideal form for a Greek revival building was the classical Greek temple, but its strict form and elaborate detail made it often poorly suited and costly to use in its pure form. The result was the practical modification and simplification of the ideal. The free-standing columns might be replaced by pilasters attached to the wall, or the full pediment might be implied by cornice returns on the gabled ends.

The largest and best-known example of the Greek revival style in Iowa is the Old Capitol in Iowa City (Fig. 40). It displays nearly all the components of the style, symmetrical composition, a gently sloping and gabled classical roof, porticos with fluted Greek Doric columns, full pediments, and entablature. The body of the building is wrapped with an entablature of the same design as that on the porticos, and pilasters continue the rhythm established by the portico columns. Because of the building's large size dictated by the diverse needs of a structure built to house a seat of government, the Greek revival character of the Old Capitol is established primarily by the decorative details of classical Greek architecture and not the classical temple form on which such details were found historically. The Lee County Courthouse in Fort Madison (Fig. M-1) displays not only the Greek architectural details, but the form of the building is the same as the temples of ancient Greece.

In order to be considered of the Greek revival style, buildings need not be as grand as the previous examples or possess all the characteristics of the style. Buildings like the Quaker Meeting House in West Branch (Fig. 50), a simple rectangular frame structure, can be said to be Greek revival primarily because of the classically-inspired roof cornice and gently sloping gable roof. The John Brown House which stood in Springdale (Figs. 33, 34) is an example of the Greek revival influence on a modestly scaled private residence. The classical pitch of the roof cornice here employs only cornice returns on the gabled building ends to suggest the roof pediments are the determining stylistic factors. The use of stucco-finished exterior walls, which are scored in a pattern to imitate regularly coursed ashlar stone construction, is an example of sophistication not usually found on such a modest structure. A large brick residence now known as Ewing Hall on the campus of Maharishi International University at Fairfield (Fig. M-2) is Greek revival because of the presence of Greek Doric columns supporting the porch roof and a classically inspired cornice. In this example the roof is hipped, not gabled, and the building mass has no resemblance to the form of the Greek temple. These examples demonstrate the diverse appearance of buildings which are Greek revival in style, diverse by virtue of shape, function, and sophistication of architectural detail. The unifying factor in these buildings is the influence of ancient Greek architecture on their architects or builders, as direct or remote as it might be.

Egyptian revival is an exotic variant of the Greek revival style and is deserving of mention in this discussion. Based on the temple architecture of ancient Egypt, it was used primarily for jails and funeral structures because of its perceived association with permanence and eternity. The prime example of the style in Iowa is the Dubuque County Jail in Dubuque (Fig. 42), with its battered walls, gorge or covered roof cornice, and columns with lotus capitals.

Primary Characteristics (1840–60)

* Gently sloping gabled roof usually with a full pediment treatment or cornice return at the gable ends.
* Generally symmetrical building composition.
* Use of the Greek classical orders (Doric, Ionic, or Corinthian) on columned porticos.
* The roof eaves are treated in a manner to suggest classical cornice or entablature.

ITALIANATE

Italianate is a broad style which includes many variations applied to almost every building type. What these variations have in common is an inspiration source in the architecture of Italy, and the tendency to use this source as a point of departure rather than as a model for duplication. Tuscan farm houses became the inspiration for country villas. Renaissance city palaces were models for banks and town houses.

One of the finest Iowa residences in the Italianate style is Hedge Hill in Burlington (Fig. M-3), with its elaborate, wide cornice and low, hipped roof. Other noteworthy features include the carved stone work, and the small entry

Fig. M-2. Fairfield. Maharishi International University. Ewing Hall.

porch. Montauk in Clermont (Fig. 56) is an example of the style, with a projecting central pavilion. The Mathias Ham House in Dubuque (Fig. M-4) and the Rensselaer Russell House in Waterloo (Fig. 36) have rooftop belvederes, another common Italianate style feature.

Other building types such as Old Main at Iowa Wesleyan College in Mt. Pleasant (Fig. 47) use many of the same stylistic details of the above houses but produce a building which appears quite different. A particularly fine Italianate county courthouse is that of Madison County in Winterset (Fig. 72). The form of the building is derived from an Italian Renaissance cruciform church with a dome over the crossing.

Primary Characteristics (1855–80)

* A square or (rarely) octagonal-shaped tower standing off-center, usually at a corner. Alternately, there may be a belvedere (cupola) at the center of the roof.

Fig. M-3. Burlington. Hedge Hill. Photo Robert Thall 1977.

* A low-pitched hip roof or, if the house has an L-shaped plan, low-pitched gable roofs might be present.
* Eaves are almost always of considerable projection, and they are usually supported by brackets.
* Usually have ashlar, brick, or clapboard exterior walls.
* Windows are often rounded on top and carry hood molds.
* Usually a wide veranda or loggia wraps around several sides of the house.
* Windows are often grouped in twos and threes.
* Bay windows and balustraded balconies are common.

Fig. M-4. Dubuque. Mathias Hamm House. Photo Jack E. Boucher 1977.

GOTHIC REVIVAL

As the name implies, the Gothic revival drew upon the architecture of the thirteenth- and fourteenth-century Europe for its inspiration. It was similar to the Greek revival in the respect that it had a perceived association with the past. To the Victorian mind, the Middle Ages were the golden age of Christianity, and in the mid-nineteenth century when the style became popular, it was frequently promoted as the only "true Christian architecture"—which accounts for the popularity of the style for church and religious buildings. But religious association alone cannot account for its popularity; Gothic detail and massing presented the architect with the opportunity for picturesque buildings, which the formality of styles such as the Greek revival had not allowed.

The influence of the Gothic revival style can be found in Iowa by the 1850s, with the best examples generally dating from the 1860s and 1870s. However, the style continued its popularity for ecclesiastical structures well into the twentieth century, and its influence may still be seen in a diluted form in some new church architecture today.

Examples of the style in Iowa are numerous, particularly in churches. One of the finest examples of the Gothic revival style in Iowa is the Trinity Episcopal Cathedral in Davenport (Figs. 70, 71). It displays all of the characteristics of the mature Gothic revival style, handled with a considerable degree of finesse. Most notably the design makes extensive use of the pointed Gothic arch motif, both on the exterior and interior. The use of stone as the primary building material is unusual as well. At the rear of the building (on the right side of the photograph), the base of the uncompleted tower is visible. At the other end of the scale of sophistication are simple vernacular frame buildings, such as "The Little Brown Church in the Vale" at Nashua (Fig. 48), which are Gothic revival style buildings because of a single design element such as the Gothic arched windows and doors.

Gothic revival style is found in a much broader range of building types than churches. A house such as the John Reichard House which stood near Knoxville (Fig. 66) was a good example of a Victorian Gothic cottage, with its pointed, arched windows, and its steeply pitched roof with elaborate barge boards trimming the gables. A large public building in the Gothic revival style was the Union Pacific Station which stood in Council Bluffs (Figs. 85, M-5). It is Gothic, despite details such as the mansard roof and corner pilasters which give the building an eclectic quality when they are grouped together with the dominating Gothic design elements.

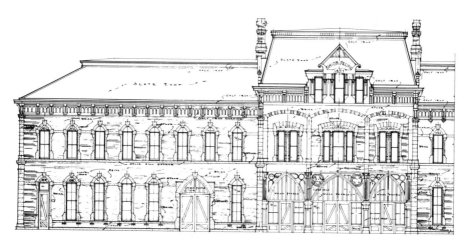

Fig. M-5. Council Bluffs. Union Pacific Depot. East elevation. Jensen-Schneider-Larson, delineators.

Primary Characteristics (1855–90)

* Pointed Gothic windows.
* Irregular and asymmetrical shape.
* Details that hang down or stand up (roof cresting, pendants, finials and the like).
* Steep-sloping gable roofs.
* Often elaborate decoration on the eaves under gables, i.e., barge boards.
* Vertical appearance.
* Picturesque and irregular massing.

SECOND EMPIRE

The Second Empire style takes its name from the reign of Napoleon III (1852–70) of France, although the forms and details of the style are based on seventeenth-century French Baroque architecture. It was not a nostalgic or romantic movement looking back, as were the Greek and Gothic revivals, but was a consciously "modern" movement, deriving its prestige from contemporary Paris. In the mid-nineteenth century Paris was considered to be one of the most modern and beautiful cities in the world, because of the massive program of Napoleon III for civic improvements and the rebuilding of large areas of the city. The architectural style used in most of this new construction is what is now known as Second Empire.

The style is most easily identified by the distinctive and often ornate mansard roof. In general Second Empire style buildings tend to reflect the feelings of optimism, individuality, and grandeur which typify the post-Civil War America.

Iowa has many fine examples which represent a great number of building types. Probably the best known in the state is Terrace Hill (Fig. 58) in Des Moines. It, like the lesser-known J. Monroe Parker House (Ficke House) (Figs. M-6, M-7) in Davenport, displays all the major characteristics and is a virtual "textbook" of the style. It is interesting to compare the two houses because they are so similar in size, stylistic details, and types of building elements. Yet each house has a distinct personality of its own. Two additional residential examples which are less opulent in detail and size are the Swain-Vincent House (Fig. 63) in Fort Dodge, and the Grenville M. Dodge House (the porch is not original to the house) (Fig. 59) in Council Bluffs.

The style was frequently employed for public buildings. The College Building (Fig. 78), which formerly stood on the campus of Iowa State University in Ames, is a prime illustration, with its elaborate mansard roof and towers capping an otherwise relatively plain building. The mansard roof is the most easily identifiable trait of the Second Empire style. However, there are buildings such as the Union Pacific Station (Fig. 85) which stood in Council Bluffs that cannot readily be considered to be Second Empire in style. The station is really Gothic revival.

Primary Characteristics (1865–85)

* Mansard roof. (A roof that has two slopes on all sides, the lower one being much steeper than the upper. A prominent curb appearing at the top of the lower slope normally obscures the view of the upper slope.)
* Houses appear tall and bold.
* Dormer windows are common and they take many different shapes.
* Chimneys are often ornately detailed, and they are important to the composition of the building.
* Buildings are often richly ornamented.

Fig. M-6. Davenport. J. Monroe Parker House (Ficke House). Photo Jack E. Boucher 1977.

RICHARDSONIAN ROMANESQUE

The Romanesque revival in America occurred in two major phases in the nineteeth century. The first phase, at mid-century, was influenced by architects Richard Upjohn and James Renwick. The second phase, popular from

135

Fig. M-7. Davenport. J. Monroe Parker House (Ficke House). Side elevation. Photo Jack E. Boucher 1977.

1880 to 1900, was largely influenced by Henry Hobson Richardson, the first American architect whose work enjoyed an international reputation. As the name implies, this style drew upon the massive stone architecture of eleventh- and twelfth-century Europe.

Although the Romanesque revival style was more suited to massive public buildings, in the Richardsonian Romanesque phase it did appear in the designs of homes of wealthy and prominent people. The Richardsonian Romanesque is noted for its rough-faced masonry, its deep-set windows, and its Roman (semicircular) arched windows and doors.

Examples of the earlier phase of this style are extremely rare in Iowa; however, the later phase is well represented in the Richardsonian Romanesque style with its massive and strong forms. The Montgomery County Courthouse (Fig. 74) in Red Oak and the Clinton County Courthouse (Fig. 75) in Clinton demonstrate this strength. The Equitable Building, now known as the Bankers Trust Building (Fig. 87), in Des Moines is an example of the Richardsonian Romanesque style applied to a high-rise office building. The shape and function of this office building may be totally different from a courthouse like the one in Montgomery County, but if one compares the use of materials and the individual details they are remarkably similar.

A particularly fine example of the Romanesque style used in a private residence is the F.D. Stout House, now the Archbishop's residence (Fig. M-8) in Dubuque. This house displaying virtually every characteristic of the Richardsonian Romanesque style was built by a wealthy industrialist in the early 1890s at a cost of more than $300,000. At that time the average house in America cost about $3,000.

Primary Characteristics (1880–1900)

* Wall surfaces are rock-faced masonry.
* Arches, lintels, and other features are often of different stone than the walls.
* Round arches are always present, but straight-topped openings are used more than in the earlier Romanesque Revival.
* Steep-gabled wall dormers may be present along with small hipped or eyebrow roof dormers.
* Chimneys are heavy, squat, and plainly treated.
* Square towers have pyramidal roofs, and round turrets and projecting bays have conical roofs.

Fig. M- 8. Dubuque. F. D. Stout House (Archbishop's Residence). Photo Jack E. Boucher 1977.

STICK STYLE

The Stick style represents an Americanized and simplified variation of the Gothic revival executed in wood and used mostly for residences. One of the most striking features of the Stick style is the attempt to reveal the structure of the building by exposing or imitating its structural members. The G. B. P.

137

Carpenter House in Burlington (Fig. M-9) displays this imaginative use of wood construction on the second floor, the porches, and in the roof gables.

Primary Characteristics (1870–90)

* Exposed stick work, either structural or applied, suggests simple reflection of inner frame. Often exposed framing especially in gable end of the roof.
* Tall proportions and high, steep roofs.
* Complex plan and irregular silhouette.
* Eaves project and are often supported by large brackets.
* Extensive verandas with the roofs carried on posts with diagonal braces.
* Usually built with clapboards having an overlay of other horizontal, vertical, and diagonal boards (sticks).

Fig. M-9. Burlington. G. B. P. Carpenter House. Courtesy of the *American Architect and Building Guide* (September 1879).

QUEEN ANNE

Unlike most other styles, the Queen Anne style was the invention of a single man, Richard Norman Shaw, a prominent English architect of the late nineteenth century. The style became popular in the United States after public exposure to the buildings erected by the British for the 1876 Philadelphia Exposition. The Queen Anne style was essentially a residential style which displayed an unrestrained exhuberance and picturesque quality. The Fannie Stout House in Dubuque (Fig. M-10) is an excellent example of the style, with a complexity of form and detail which virtually defies description.

138

Primary Characteristics (1880–95)

* Asymmetrical and irregular plan and massing.
* Variety of roof types, surface textures, and wall projections.
* Windows take many forms, straight-topped or round-arched, but not pointed. Double-hung sashes often feature many small lights over a single light.
* Bay windows and rounded or polygonal turrets are common.
* Details are usually classical and tend to be small in scale, thus heightening the over-all effect of complexity.
* Sometimes clapboards and shingles are used above a brick or stone first story.
* Roofs are steep and multiple, frequently intersecting.
* Gables often form right-angled triangles with the aid of a cornice or pent roof.
* Elaborate and large chimneys are important features.

Fig. M-10. Dubuque. Fannie Stout House. Photo Jack E. Boucher 1977.

139

SHINGLE

Related to the Queen Anne is the American Shingle style, which is relatively rare in Iowa. Like the Queen Anne, it is a residential style. Its tendency is also toward irregular massing, with bays and projects from the facade. One of the distinguishing features of the style is the use of shingles, particularly on vertical wall surfaces. The Mrs. D. B. Sutherland House in Council Bluffs (Fig. M-11) is typical of the Shingle style in Iowa.

Primary Characteristics (1885–1900)

* Appears more horizontal than the Stick or Queen Anne styles.
* Exterior wall to upper stories at least, and often the ground story, have a uniform covering of shingles.
* When the lowest story is not shingled, it is usually of stone.
* Windows have small lights and often form horizontal bands.
* Roofs may be hipped, gable, or gambrel, or a combination of these forms.
* Roof pitch is more moderate than Queen Anne.
* Segmental bays and round turrets are common.

COTTAGE at COUNCIL BLUFFS. IOWA. for MRS D.B.SUTHERLAND.   JHackett Kent Architect

Fig. M-11. Council Bluffs. Mrs. D. B. Sutherland House. Courtesy of the *Inland Architect and News Record* (May 1892).

PRAIRIE

The Prairie style is America's only architectural style developed in the Midwest specifically for the Midwest. Its master was Frank Lloyd Wright, one of the nation's most noted architects. "We of the Middle West," he wrote, "are living on the prairie. The prairie has a beauty of its own and we should recognize and accentuate this natural beauty, its quiet level. Hence, gently sloping roofs, low proportions, quiet sky lines, suppressed heavy-set chimneys and sheltering overhangs, low terraces and out-reaching walls sequestering private gardens."

Emerging just before the turn of the century, the Prairie style foreshadowed much modern residential architecture. Perhaps one of the most striking features of the Prairie style home is its sense of age, often appearing to have been built recently instead of in 1915.

Iowa has numerous excellent examples of the Prairie style, executed by many of the leading architects of the period. One of the finest examples in Iowa as well as the United States is the City National Bank and Park Inn Hotel in Mason City (Fig. 98). This building by Wright displays all the distinctive characteristics of the style, with a particularly strong emphasis on the horizontal lines of the building in its roof eaves, bands of windows, and balconies. A similar feeling is evident in the Arthur Rule House, also in Mason City (Fig. 99), designed by Walter Burley Griffin, or in the James Clarke House in Fairfield (Fig. 104), designed by Francis Barry Byrne. The Prairie style influence can also be seen in buildings of a more conventional appearance, such as the J. B. Butler House in Fort Dodge (Fig. M-12), with its strong horizontal lines and areas of concentrated ornament.

Fig. M-12. Fort Dodge. J. B. Butler House. Photo Robert Thall 1977.

Although the Prairie style was most frequently employed for residences, there are excellent non-residential examples in Iowa. The previously mentioned bank and hotel in Mason City is only one example. Another is the Merchants' National Bank in Grinnell (Fig. 95), designed by Louis Sullivan. Contrary to the previous examples, this building is not dominantly horizontal in feeling. A major feature is the use of richly detailed ornament of an original and frequently organic character, which is concentrated around doors, windows, and roof line.

The most unique building of the Prairie style in Iowa is the Woodbury County Courthouse in Sioux City (Fig. 101), designed by Purcell and Elmslie. It is the only large civic structure to be executed in the Prairie style in the United States.

Of all the styles included in this guide, the Prairie style is the most individualistic and the most difficult to categorize. It is unified by the idea of creating a distinctly midwestern architecture rather than a notion of what a building should look like.

Primary Characteristics (1900–15)

* Dominant horizontal lines.
* Organically inspired ornament usually centered around and on building features such as windows, doors, and columns.
* Two stories—occasionally three—often with single-story wings projecting in more than one direction.
* Carports or porches at ends of wings, with their roofs as extensions of the main house roof.
* Each wing usually contains a single large room. In general, the entire interior effect emphasizes openness.
* Low roofs, often hipped, with extremely wide eave projections and an overall horizontal emphasis.
* Dormers are seldom used.
* Ribbon windows, belt courses, and dark wood stripping along the sill line emphasize horizontality.
* Sometimes vertical wood stripping or half-timbering effects are found.
* Exterior surface usually plaster (stucco) or brick. Combinations of different materials shunned in favor of non-conflicting exterior materials.

ENGLISH TUDOR

The first third of this century saw the rise of the eclectic revivals, particularly in residential architecture. The eclectic revival styles attempted to copy the architectural appearance of various historic styles to the greatest practical degree, while still allowing for functional floor plans and other twentieth-century comforts, such as modern plumbing and central heating.

The English Tudor style became one of the main forces in this eclectic revival in the early part of the twentieth century. It derives its name from the Tudor monarchs, Henry VII through Elizabeth I, who ruled England during the fifteenth and sixteenth centuries. Unlike many other styles which maintained regional differences, the English Tudor style remained remarkably consistent wherever it arose. A prime example of the style is the Ralph Rollins House (Fig. M-13) in Des Moines.

Primary Characteristics (1910–35)

* Irregular plans, usually two stories with wings often going off at oblique angles.
* Half-timbering is the most noticeable feature on the exterior walls, although it is often only a design feature with no structural value.
* Roofs are very steep.
* Chimneys are decorative, often with a chimney pot.
* Tudor (four-centered) arches are common over entries, and occasionally over windows.
* Frequent use of grouped windows; often with leaded glass panes.

Fig. M-13. Des Moines. Ralph Rollins House. Photo Robert Thall 1977.

GEORGIAN REVIVAL

The Georgian revival, another of the eclectic revival styles, branched into two major substyles. One revived details of the Adam style of eighteenth-century England. The other revived the American Georgian Colonial tradition. It is this second branch of the Georgian revival that is most prominent in Iowa.

With the Georgian revival in the first third of the twentieth century symmetry again became an important characteristic in American residential architec-

143

ture for the first time since the Greek revival more than a half-century before. The Georgian revival emphasized formality, order, and a regal simplicity. It rejected the horizontality of the Prairie style, the modesty of the Bungalow, and especially the lavish complexity of the Queen Anne and its related traditions. The W. W. Witmer House (former governor's mansion) (Fig. M-14) in Des Moines exemplifies this style.

Primary Characteristics (1900–40)

* Symmetrical facades.
* Rectangular in plan with a minimum of projections.
* Roofs are hipped, double-pitched, or gambrel with eaves detailed as classical cornices.
* Hipped roof often has a flat top with a surrounding railing or balustrade.
* Roof dormers are frequent.
* Chimneys add to over-all symmetry.
* Central part of the facade may project slightly and may be crowned with a pediment supported by pilasters.
* Occasionally a portico with free-standing columns may be present. The classical details are inspired by Roman rather than Greek models.
* Doorways have fanlights or pedimented frames.
* Double-hung sash is normal, but palladian windows occasionally appear for emphasis.

Fig. M-14. Des Moines. W. W. Witmer House (former governor's mansion). Courtesy of the *Western Architect* (February 1906).

MEDITERRANEAN

As the English Tudor and the Georgian revival attempted to recreate the details of an earlier architecture, so to did the Mediterranean style, which adopted its design from Spanish and Italian buildings of the Middle Ages.

Although the Mediterranean style is not perfectly suited to the ravages of an Iowa winter, there are, nevertheless, a number of examples, such as the James E. Hamilton House (Fig. M-15) in Cedar Rapids, to be found around the state.

Primary Characteristics (1910–35)

* White stucco finished walls.
* Low-pitched roofs with tile, usually red.
* An emphasis on open space. Patios, courts, and open galleries are prominent features, although they are necessarily limited in Iowa due to the weather.
* Basic Spanish and Italian design motifs.
* Black wrought-iron window grilles and heavy wooden shutters stand out against the light-colored brick or stucco walls.
* Semicircular window arches and other semicircular features.

Fig. M-15. Cedar Rapids. James E. Hamilton House. Photo Robert Thall 1977.

BUNGALOW

Soon after the Prairie style developed in the Midwest, another twentieth-century residential style—the Bungalow—began sweeping the country from west to east. Devised in California and spread eastward by magazines in the teens and twenties, the Bungalow, although less aesthetically important than the Prairie style, became far more popular and affordable to working-class Americans. Examples of this modest style can be seen in practically every community. The Melrose Day Care Center at 701 Melrose Avenue (Fig. M-16) in Iowa City is typical of the style.

Primary Characteristics (1910–30)

* Simple horizontal lines.
* Always a small, modest home.
* Always a single story, although there may be a single dormer, and, perhaps, windows in the gables. (Houses with second stories can be "bungaloid" or "built along Bungalow lines," but are never true Bungalows.)
* Projecting eaves that usually show exposed rafter ends.
* One or two large porches.
* Prominent chimney—often built of rubble.
* Protruding brackets often used as decorative features.
* Usually wood siding (horizontal or vertical) with wood shingles, logs, stones, brick, or stucco veneer for a rustic look.

Fig. M-16. Iowa City. Melrose Day Care Center. Photo Hans Muessig 1978.

BEAUX ARTS CLASSICISM

The name of this style comes from the École des Beaux Arts in Paris, the most renowned architectural school in the world at the end of the nineteenth century, where many outstanding American architects of this period had been educated. The style called upon Roman imperial architecture, usually with some influence from seventeenth- and eighteenth-century French architecture, as a model for its buildings, and achieved a truly popular influence as a result of the World's Columbian Exhibition in Chicago in 1893. All of the buildings at the exhibition were executed in the Beaux Arts style, presenting one of the grandest architectural vistas ever seen in America. The buildings caused the fair to be christened "The White City."

The influence of "The White City" spread far afield, becoming the popular style for public, civic, and banking buildings. One of the finest examples in Iowa is the Polk County Courthouse in Des Moines (Figs. 89, 90). Both the inside and outside of the building display a richness and flamboyance of classical architectural detail. The Kendall Young Library in Webster City (Fig. M-17) is a small scale but equally good example of the Beaux Arts style, with its highly ornamented front entry.

Primary Characteristics (1895–1920)

* Usually built primarily of dressed and highly detailed stone exterior.
* Elements of classical Roman architecture are present, such as columns, pilasters, arches, classical cornices, and decorative carvings of garlands or trophies.
* Symmetrical composition with the center always visually dominant, sometimes with central domes or towers.

Fig. M-17. Webster City. Kendall Young Library. Courtesy of the *Inland Architect and News Record* (March 1904).

147

MODERNE/ART DECO

The Moderne or Art Deco style represented a desire to create a twentieth-century style. Architects were trying to break with the historical styles and to create one which represented "The Modern Age," as they saw it. The Earl Butler House in Des Moines (Fig. M-18) attempts this by the use of new building materials. Poured in place structural concrete and metal windows were used in a way to suggest a streamlined modernity. It is interesting to note that the transition between architectural styles was far from absolute at a given time; the Butler House and the Rollins House (Fig. M-13) are located next to each other and both were built in 1928.

A second Iowa example of the Moderne style is the *Press Citizen* newspaper office building in Iowa City (Fig. M-19), which does not strip away all decoration. Rather it uses decorative relief panels showing designs of trains, airplanes, and other twentieth-century wonders.

Primary Characteristics (1925–40)

* Absence of traditional architectural ornament and detail.
* A tendency to make the building appear to be streamlined.
* Use of new building materials such as concrete, metal window frames, and glass block.
* Usually flat roofs.

Fig. M-18. Des Moines. Earl Butler House. Photo Robert Thall 1977.

Fig. M-19. Iowa City. Iowa City *Press Citizen* Building. Photo Hans Muessig 1978.

Index

Note: Cities are in Iowa, unless otherwise indicated. The Appendix and the Bibliographic Essay are not indexed.

Wright, Frank Lloyd, 1, 67, 70, 71, 75, 77, 107, 108, 141

Young, Alexander, House, Washington, 7

Zion, Old Church, Burlington. *See* Methodist Episcopal Church of Burlington